JACK LEVINE

Photograph by Virginia G. Schendler, 1988

JACK LEVINE

Commentary by
JACK LEVINE

Introduction by
MILTON W. BROWN

Compiled and edited by
STEPHEN ROBERT FRANKEL

RIZZOLI
NEW YORK

A Chameleon Book

First published in the United States of America in 1989 by
RIZZOLI INTERNATIONAL PUBLICATIONS, INC.
300 Park Avenue South, New York, NY 10010

Produced by Chameleon Books, Inc.
211 West 20th Street
New York, NY 10011

Production director/designer: Arnold Skolnick
Editorial director: Marion Wheeler
Associate editor: Stephen Robert Frankel
Composition: Ultracomp, New York
Production services: Four Colour Imports, Ltd., Louisville, Kentucky
Printed and bound by Everbest Printing Company, Ltd., Hong Kong

Library of Congress Cataloging-in-Publication Data

Jack Levine/introduction by Milton W. Brown; commentary by Jack Levine;
  commentary compiled and edited by Stephen Robert Frankel.
  p. cm.
  ISBN 0-8478-0977-3
  1. Levine, Jack, 1915-   —Catalogs. I. Levine, Jack, 1915-
  II. Brown, Milton Wolf, 1911-   . III. Frankel, Stephen Robert.
  N6537.L45A4 1989
  759. 13—dc20

88-42699 CIP

CONTENTS

Foreword 7

Introduction 9

Biographical Outline 17

The Early Years 18

The '40s 34

The '50s 50

The '60s 93

The '70s 110

The '80s 127

Source Notes 140

Public Collections 140

Exhibitions 141

Bibliography 142

Index 144

ACKNOWLEDGMENTS

Chameleon Books gratefully acknowledges the generous assistance in providing photographs by Fred Bernaski, The Kennedy Galleries; Jonathan Bergen, The ACA Galleries; Bridget Moore, The Midtown Galleries; and all those wonderful people at the public institutions.

Acknowledgment and thanks are also owed to photographers Toby Old, Robert E. Mates, Ed Watkins, and Bill O'Connor; and to the private collectors, who provided ready access to Jack Levine's work.

We wish to thank David Sutherland; who gave us permission to use a transcript of the film *JACK LEVINE: Feast of Pure Reason* and to quote portions of it in the text.

We offer special thanks to Milton W. Brown for his contribution, to Susanna Levine Fisher for her generous assistance; and especially to Stephen Robert Frankel who made great order out of chaos in putting together the wonderful text from so many diverse sources, and for his insight and professionalism.

Finally we wish to thank Jack Levine, who gave his valuable time and shared his wisdom.

Foreword

by JACK LEVINE

ST. JEROME 1930
Graphite on off-white paper, 13¹¹⁄₁₆ x 9⅞ in.
Fogg Art Museum, Harvard University, Cambridge, Mass.
Bequest of Dr. Denman W. Ross, 1975

Mastery over the image is the prerequisite to the artist's mission, the elevation of the human race. As I look over the history of art, which is to say, to look beyond the immediate work of the 20th century, it appears to me that from the most ancient times, power over the image was central in the activities of the artist.

Consider the cave painter in prehistoric times. We do not know how his skills evolved but we do know that this process of ideation and transfer took place. Otherwise, one must conjecture a cave filled with mammoths and aurochs demurely posing for immortalization into the millennia. The cave artist conjured up images which were magical to his audience. To them, the images promoted successful hunting and seemingly enhanced their power over nature. Many years ago, I read a passage by Frans Boaz, which stated that in the paleolithic period, when man hunted, when man lived in an epic phase, the art was figurative in character. It was during the neolithic period subsequent to the paleolithic, according to Boaz, that we began to see artifacts and implements which had decorative embellishments and, one might say, an abstract character which developed out of a more truncated existence.

I think we may begin, then, with the high purpose of the artist priest. The survival of his people, the success of the hunt or of the crop, the glory of God, sermons on ethics, morality, the joy of life, and the tragedy of death—all of these have been manifested at various times in human history by the artist. The public need for meaningful symbols, then, whether in a cave or cathedral, gave rise to this substantive character which arose from the artist's mind.

Such is the power of the image created by the artist that my own faith, that of the Jews, at times looked upon it with suspicion. Image making was, by turns, prohibited or certainly inhibited. This undoubtedly accounts for the absence of Jews in the history of art until some time in the 18th century. But an indication of difference of interpretation is evidenced by frescoes of great antiquity found in the synagogue at Dura-Europos and the mosaic floor of the Beth Alpha Synagogue in Israel.

Hellenic art rests on the idealization of the human body and in its elevation to divinity. Phidias, much of whose life was spent among athletes striving at the palaestra, needed only a canon of proportion and an anatomical sense to shape and analyze his inner conception. Does not the mythologist convey all this in his legends of Pygmalion and Galatea? Pygmalion chips away at the marble block to attain the image of his ideal beloved. As the marble turns from white to rose she pulses and comes to life. What if, as Pygmalion embraces her, she turns and catches sight of the model? It would be an interesting ménage à trois but it would not be the art of creation about which we are talking.

The icon painters and the primitives of the early international style worked on the basis of the copy book and emulation of pre-existing paintings by the master. We know that the assistants and apprentices in the old *botteghe* succeeded their masters as artists. They trained by grinding colors and grounding panels and canvases. They traced, perforated, pounced, and transferred designs. As they developed, they were entrusted with laying in the preliminary painting for the master. When their skills warranted, they were accepted into the guild of St. Luke and they became full-fledged artists in the community. Generations of artists evolved in this fashion.

With the rediscovery of classical art and the growing humanism, the artist felt the need for knowledge of anatomy, perspective, aerial perspective, and optics. It involved, in other words, all the laws that would enable the artist to

This essay was written as a speech which I called "In Praise of Knowledge" and delivered in the Hall of the Synod at the Vatican in July 1976, for a seminar on "The Influence of Spiritual Inspiration on American Art" (sponsored jointly by the Vatican Museums and the Smithsonian Institution, and organized by the Galleria d'Arte Religiosa Moderna dei Musei Vaticani and the Committee of Religion and Art in America).

set down his dreams in a way which was absolutely convincing to the beholder. These complex schemata enabled the artist to achieve his purpose without reference to any immediate model. These studies were vital to Alberti's concept of *istoria* and still exist in art schools as a vestigial appendage.

Michelangelo's frescoes in the Sistine Chapel were possible because of this knowledge and this science. It was the scaffolding without which his mighty utterance would not have been possible. I do not deny that he availed himself of a model from time to time. That is a matter of record. But to think the frescoes a collage of life studies would be fatuous indeed.

As a matter of fact, there is a delightful description in *The Drawings of the Venetian Painters* by Hans Tietze and E. Tietze-Conrat of a device employed by Tintoretto and his school. A shadow-box was constructed, the floor of which was marked off as a checkerboard to plot the perspective. Figures were modeled in wax or clay and arranged in depth much as a stage director or a choreographer might do. Infinite care was paid to the facings—that is to say, the front view, side and rear, and three-quarter aspects, and all the degrees between. Heavenly figures were suspended from the roof of the box much as in the Christmas *presepi* I used to see at Naples. A candle served as a dramatic directional illumination. The Tietzes add that Tintoretto would set his students the problem of revising an established composition by retaining the silhouettes of the figures but reversing their aspects. That is to say, a figure front view would become rear view, three-quarter front would become three-quarter rear and vice-versa, profiles being immutable. The challenge was to make a coherent tableau. With this aid, effects were achieved which otherwise seem beyond the reach of invention.

I cite this as an example of a playful imaginative aid to study which gave Tintoretto a stage manager's command of new dramatic possibilities. But I have been repelled by vulgarized accounts of Leonardo walking in the streets of Milan looking for an ideal model for his Christ in the *Last Supper* or his Judas. Just think—Leonardo, the man who created what the great director Sergei Eisenstein considered a glorious film script for a deluge. The man who described looking at cracked walls to see images in them, the man who studied, as Michelangelo did, all the areas of empirical science that controlled the appearances of things, so that he could take command of them—imagine an artist like Leonardo da Vinci searching in the street for a type, instead of projecting his own inner concept of what such a man would look like.

Michelangelo was as concerned with the condition of man, his life, his aspirations, his death, and the decay of the flesh as was Dante. We are still prone to disparage the artist because of the earthbound nature of the materials with which he works. Great art rises above the material and is a mission to humanity.

The command of language, the stretching of the artist's capacities, the use of science—all of these are necessary for the main purpose, that of the elevation of man.

Rembrandt, whose powers of human empathy and psychic transference go beyond analysis, shared with the other painters of the Lowlands that joy in the richness of material substances and in the texture of the paint he used to transfigure them. Without question he worked from nature, and inventories of his house list his ownership of jewelry, armor, and precious brocades. And there were identifiable models, beginning with his parents, and including Saskia, Hendrickje Stoffels, and many others. But there are pen sketches by Rembrandt, compositions with twenty or more figures which were drawn in four or five minutes. These are not paste-ups of other figures done from life. There are sketches of figures done from nature which we find repeated in the "Hundred Gulder Print," but many other figures arise impromptu on the copper plate.

Perhaps the definitive Rembrandt for me is *The Return of the Prodigal Son* in the Hermitage. It is the highest drama I know. The blind old father stands facing us, his hands on the Prodigal's shoulders. The Prodigal kneels on the bare stone floor, his clothes are rags and patches, his bare feet dirty and travel-worn. The paint is applied smoothly with the fingers, coarsely with thick bristles, it is heaped on with the trowel. The background is in liquid transparencies of infinite depth. It is an expression of the most elevated grandeur and is at the same time terrestrial and earthy.

I know I have talked at some length about the past. The history of art is very important to me. But since I am here as a painter I feel I should tell you about my background and my approach to painting. Schools of the past took hundreds of years to develop. They grew slowly, organically. But in my time, everything accelerated. In my boyhood, I had the privilege of studying with Denman W. Ross, an Impressionist theorist and a connoisseur of Oriental art who had worked with Monet at Giverny. My association with Ross was around 1928 when Americans in Paris were imitating Cézanne still-lifes, and Cubism was a recently accomplished thing. Later, as a child of the Depression, I was attracted to so-called social painting, the Mexican fresco painters and the violently psychological German Expressionists. From the age of ten onward I had trained to draw from imagination or memory and was equipped to deal with dramatic ideas. I had at my majority been a professional artist for five years. I had had my own studio and devoted all my time to painting.

Just before World War II, in the United States, the movements were American regionalism, social realism, Surrealism, and there was a growing interest in abstract art. During the time I served in the army the Abstract Expressionist movement was developing. By 1950, it really took over. This dominance lasted about 15 years. It was succeeded by New Image of Man—pop art, kinetic, conceptual, minimal, hard-edge, collage, découpage, environmental and earth art, photo realism, and, most recently, photography itself.

Nothing can evolve organically at this rate of speed. This proliferation of movements can only produce ephemera. I am alienated from all these movements. They offer me nothing. I think of myself as a dramatist. I look for a dramatic situation which may or may not reflect some current political social response on my part and I improvise the characters as I am painting. On my release from the army, I painted *Welcome Home*, a satire on a general returning from the wars. I painted *Reception in Miami* as an expression of distaste for the bowing and scraping and fawning of Americans upon seeing the Duke and Duchess of Windsor in a hotel lobby. Shocked by the execution of the Rosenbergs, which evoked protest all over the world, including the intercession of Pope Pius XII, I painted *The Trial*, meaning to express anger at this monstrous event. I was, however, curtailed by the realization that the Warren Supreme Court was at that time our only hope for a liberal free society. *The Trial* remains a political statement, ambivalent and tentative in its utterance. It is designed in boxlike units and has a claustrophobic feeling about it.

I painted a *Witches' Sabbath* about McCarthyism and the so-called "pumpkin conspiracy," and *The Patriarch of Moscow on a Trip to Jerusalem*, a work with heavy overtones of a Russian opera, comic and sinister by turns. My painting *Cain and Abel* (which is in the Vatican) is, of course, an anti-war statement. But I am not without my tender moments, and throughout the years I have done a long series of miniatures of kings and sages of Israel, as well as a number of gentle paintings of young girls.

It is obvious that Europe has been my training ground. I tried to form myself in the great European tradition. I visit often to be refreshed by the museums, churches, and galleries. But it seems apparent from the descriptions of some of the things I have done that I am very much an American.

I am primarily concerned with the condition of man. The satirical direction I have chosen is an indication of my disappointment in man, which is the opposite way of saying that I have high expectations for the human race.

Introduction

by MILTON W. BROWN

THE FEAST OF PURE REASON 1937
(Illustrated in color on page 101, with commentary by Jack Levine)

Jack Levine is one of the major American artists of this century. He is also remarkably articulate about art, which is somewhat unusual among artists, and is possessed of a wry wit that can impale a quarry's cant and hypocrisy with epigrammatic felicity, a mocking humor that he sometimes turns rather disarmingly on himself. Above all, Levine is very clear in his own mind as to what he is about. He has the highest ideals about his vocation—and it is unquestionably a vocation—balanced by a surprisingly practical approach to it. He is, as you will soon discover for yourself, if you haven't already looked at the pictures, a representational painter, and a social one to boot, a member of an embattled species in recent decades. He has the psychic scars to show for it, and he does so quite descriptively and with some rancor. It makes for interesting reading, for Levine is not averse to being explicit in identifying his opposition; he pulls no punches, and he is picturesque in his invective. Aside from his avowed dissatisfaction with the state of the world in general, he is vastly annoyed at the treatment that social art has received at the hands of the art establishment, and the effect that it has had on his own position and reputation.

Jack Levine arrived on the American art scene in 1937 in the middle of the Depression with his painting *The Feast of Pure Reason.* "Arrived" is something of an understatement. He exploded like a skyrocket as an artistic prodigy at the age of 22 and was immediately established in the ranks of those who were then called Social Realists. You can learn more of the details of his life, and from a more reliable source, in his own account in the following pages. I am interested here rather in placing him in historic context.

During the years of crisis from the stock market crash of 1929 to the bombing of Pearl Harbor in 1941, the United States was racked by unprecedented economic, ideological, and cultural tensions. There has never been a time in our history when artists were so personally affected by physical need, so involved in economic action, so moved to political expression and organization, or so caught up in aesthetic debate. It was a time of intellectual ferment, questioning, daring, a time of economic solidarity and ideological factionalism. The Depression engendered unique social and cultural responses in the United States, including a drawing back from international affairs and a concentration on internal problems of economic survival.

This national crisis had an inadvertent and unforeseen positive effect on American culture through emergency government support of the arts on an unprecedented scale under a series of agencies, especially the Works Project Administration (WPA) from 1935 to 1943. As part of the Roosevelt administration's effort to cope with unemployment and economic stagnation, qualified individuals who were on the relief rolls were assigned to cultural projects in their field—music, theater, dance, literature, the fine arts, and crafts. Under the guise of "make work" projects, which opponents called "boondoggling," the creative forces of the nation were mobilized for the first time in our history to spread and popularize all the arts through performance, exhibition, and instruction. Never have so many artists of all kinds been gainfully employed, though salaries were minimal and tenure uncertain. The numbers involved in this entire process of creation and consumption are incalculable. Suffice it to say that under the Federal Art Project (FAP) alone, an estimated 3,600 artists produced 16,000 works that were shown in 1,000 cities and towns.

Aside from the work produced, which for a half century has generally been dismissed out of hand or treated with embarrassment, the FAP served as a training ground for a generation of artists, raised the entire level of professional competence among them, and, in throwing them together, helped foster a consciousness of art and artists as a function of society. The times were not easy and circumstances far from pleasant. Being on relief was itself demeaning, and the specter of the "pink slip" of dismissal hovered over all. Existence was snarled and time consumed by red tape and petty bureaucratic annoyances,

OAK STREET 1959
(Illustrated in color on page 90, with commentary by Jack Levine on page 91)

as well as by larger uncertainties, and by union actions, demonstrations, and factional quarrels. But the vitality that permeated the art scene, the camaraderie among artists, was unique in American history. It was in this environment that Jack Levine emerged as an artist.

In this climate, American artists were, in a sense, being impelled economically and ideologically into a new social responsibility. By accepting public support, they were expected to respond to public sentiment and taste. During the same years, the worldwide crisis was leading the United States into a period of isolationism and increased nationalism. Cultural nationalism in this country had already burgeoned directly after World War I, when the United States had achieved a new international hegemony. A search for the American ethos had begun in the '20s and then gathered impetus in the '30s, exemplified by a return to the American subject and to realism, after an interlude of experimentation with what was perceived as "foreign" modernism. The temporary revival of the earlier Ashcan tradition of realism in the '20s, the emergence of a new "American Scene" painting in the work of such artists as Edward Hopper and Charles Burchfield, followed by the Regionalism of Thomas H. Benton, Grant Wood, and John Steuart Curry, prepared the way for the social art of the '30s. Modernism was hardly dead, but representational art had returned to dominance, at least for a time.

These developments of the '20s, which should be subsumed under the general rubric of social art, continued into the '30s. The "urban realism" exemplified by such followers of Kenneth Hayes Miller as Reginald Marsh, Edward Laning, and Isabel Bishop, as well as the Soyer brothers (Moses, Raphael, and Isaac), among others, was essentially an extension of the Ashcan tradition of urban genre art. The interest of such artists was in the life of the city and its streets, in the lower classes, in the recognizable activities and amusements of "the masses," observed with realistic detail as life rather than art. But recording aspects of everyday life at a time of economic crisis—scenes of idleness, depression, poverty, breadlines, and unemployment—seemed more relevant than the happier and more positive view of life that had interested the Ashcan painters, so that many urban realist works appeared to carry more social content than was intended, while in other cases more was implied than expressed.

There was a fine, sometimes almost invisible line of distinction between Social Realism and Urban Realism. In the former, the social comment was understood to be conscious, more pointed, and the formal expression ranged beyond the confines of naturalism into symbolism, expressionism, and even surrealism. Social Realism did not dominate the art of the period, but it was at least for a time the eye of aesthetic controversy. It served to polarize artistic attitudes by postulating the premises of social relevance and communication as requisites of art. The more radical, Marxist-oriented artists of the John Reed Club saw all art as an expression of class struggle, from which it followed that the conscious artist had to accept the consequences of his political and social allegiance. And, since art was a weapon in the class struggle, to be most effective it must be communicative on the broadest levels. Of course, many artists did not accept the political convictions or the philosophical arguments of the Marxists, and many who did refused to equate art with propaganda.

In the ensuing battle over ideology, the Social Realists attacked the Regionalists for what they considered to be reactionary social attitudes, wrote off the majority of artists for their political obtuseness or lack of commitment at a time of world crisis, and inveighed against abstract and avant-garde art in general as social and cultural retreat into an ivory tower. However, the polemics were not one-sided. The Regionalists reviled the Social Realists and Modernists equally as alien, decadent, and subversive of American traditions and values. And the Modernists dismissed representation in art as irrelevant and, more specifically, Regionalism as illustration and Social Realism as propaganda. The heat of argument was symptomatic of the social climate. There was much discussion about art and reality and the role of art and artists in society. These were questions of profound significance and, in the face of mounting international tensions, it is not surprising that artists and other intellectuals of various persuasions rallied to support the Artists' Congress in 1936. External, political circumstances had forced a sense of unity on the intellectual community, at least for a while.

Historical circumstances—the world in an economic depression, the threat of war and Fascism, the Spanish Civil War—appeared to be vindicating the political and, by inference, the artistic position of the left and to enhance the status of Social Realism. Some artists, for whom it had not been usual before, now turned to social comment in their art, among them Max Weber, Peter Blume, and Philip Guston, to name only some of the better known. There were many others who made a passing stab at social art almost as a social imperative, and some were listed in the ranks of Social Realism because their work seemed to imply social intentions. The major artists identified with Social Realism, in addition to Jack Levine, were Ben Shahn, Philip Evergood, William Gropper, Jacob Lawrence, Robert Gwathmey, Anton Refregier, and Joseph Hirsch. Others, less well known, were Mervin Jules, Harry Sternberg, Charles White, Harry Gottlieb, Honoré Sharrer, and Walter Quirt, some of whom faded from view as the movement declined and tastes changed, while others shifted allegiance and later appeared in rival camps. For a time, Social Realism had widespread impact, extending beyond the Eastern seaboard to the West and weaning away from Regionalism a younger generation of artists—including Joe Jones, James Turnbull, Mitchell Siporin, and Edward Millman. The Social Realists all shared a common desire to use their art for social ends and were drawn together in common activity on the projects, around the John Reed Club, the Artists' Union, and the Artists' Congress, but there was no expressive or aesthetic consensus among them. Social Realism ran the gamut from the heroic to the ironic, from the satiric to the sentimental, from the passionate to the cerebral, from cliché to fantasy, from the fringes of Cubism to those of Surrealism, from naturalism to symbolism, covering a range of styles that included all the current modes just this side of nonobjectivism.

Social Realism as a force in American art did not outlive the war, although some artists remained loyal to its fundamental precepts and continued to work in that vein beyond the '40s, in spite of the political atmosphere of the Cold War and McCarthyism, and a hostile aesthetic environment. The decline of the movement resulted from a variety of factors: the political debacle of the left, following the Nazi-Soviet Pact, and the attendant disillusionment of many artists with the Soviet Union, Communism, or even political commitment as such, which led, among other things, to the collapse of the Artists' Congress; the easing of the Depression and phasing out of the WPA; the increasing impact of avant-garde art fostered by the influx of artist refugees from Hitler and the war; and the war itself, which in its anti-Fascist character, blunted criticism from any quarter.

Although Surrealism had a profound effect on the development of Abstract Expressionism in the '40s, it had had very little currency in the United States before that. However, its free and imaginative use of imagery and symbols did attract some artists who were interested in social themes, such as Peter Blume, O. Louis Guglielmi, Walter Quirt, James Guy, and the sculptor David Smith. The work of Philip Evergood often carries overtones of Surrealism. Surrealism at least suggested the possibility of making bold ideological statements in symbolic and more personal terms, unrestricted by the exigencies of naturalism, history, or the unities of time and space. However, such Social Surrealists, unlike "classical" Surrealists, were not necessarily committed to Freudian symbolism and avoided purely unconscious or irrational relationships among pictorial elements. The connections were intended to be socially meaningful, if not entirely explicit, so that Social Surrealism is sometimes closer to Symbolism than to Surrealism.

THE SPANISH PRISON 1959–62
(Illustrated on page 28, with commentary by Jack Levine on page 29)

1932 (IN MEMORY OF GEORGE GROSZ) 1959
(Illustrated in color on page 87, with commentary by Jack Levine)

Located somewhere between Realism and Surrealism, neither prosaic enough for the former nor irrational enough for the latter, was an ill-defined phenomenon called "Magic Realism," which had much in common with German *Neue Sachlichkeit* and French Neo-Romanticism without being a direct counterpart of either. It was unmistakably American, its subject matter native and popular, prefiguring Pop Art in its fascination with iconic trivia. It was never a cohesive movement, but rather a sack into which were dumped disparate but somehow related artists who were difficult to pigeonhole, encompassing, for instance, the obsessive morbidity of Ivan Albright, the brooding asceticism of Andrew Wyeth, the frenetic social satire of Paul Cadmus, the frustrating ambiguities of Jared French, and the poetic mysticism of Edwin Dickinson. Magic Realism was an eccentric realism with tangential social relevance, finding the unexpected in the commonplace, fantasy in the prosaic, the undecipherable in the apparent. It called a change on American subject painting by inverting accepted notions of significance, and it offered representational artists dissatisfied with the parameters of Regionalism, Urban Realism, or Social Realism the possibility of philosophical or psychological meaning beyond the explicit.

It was into this aesthetic maelstrom that Jack Levine's art first surfaced, although he was then still physically in Boston. However, the government projects were operating in all the large cities, and the art magazines kept the hinterlands conversant with what was new. In 1937, when the Museum of Modern Art acquired *The Feast of Pure Reason,* he achieved instant national recognition. I can remember the impression it made at the time, at least on me, as something fresh and original, unlike any of the Social Realist art we were used to. It seemed very American in its streetwise urban iconography and it was painted with a brassy bravura that still bowed to all the corners of traditional art. Unfortunately, his career was interrupted by the war, but the purchase of his *String Quartet,* by the Metropolitan Museum of Art, while he was still in the army, reinforced his reputation as a bright new star in the American artistic firmament. Looking back at that time, he can say with rueful wryness, "I made quite a splash in the art world in the 1930s when I was just a kid, and it seems to me that every year since, I have become less and less well known." Despite this stoical dismissal of his reputation, which is in a sense accurate enough, he has left an indelible mark on his time.

In my experience, all artists hate to be labeled. They seem to believe with almost primitive superstition that if you identify them, their art will somehow lose its magic or, if you attach them to a movement, they will lose their individuality. Art historians, however, like to put artists, all artists, in slots, because they become easier to define, understand, and handle. Levine is different in that he willingly admits to being a social artist, even a Social Realist. But that category is so encompassing that his art calls for more precise definition. And here, as an art historian *manqué,* he pretty well defines himself as a history painter and a satirist.

History painting is an ancient and revered category in the history of art, and, as Jack aptly points out, at one time the highest order of painting, an opinion that he still endorses. History painting is literary or story-telling art. Its sources are the mythology, literature, and history of humanity in its myriad guises and symbolic forms. Most of Social Realist painting dealt with contemporary everyday events and situations and is thus genre rather than history painting. But history has an added resonance in Levine's art. His relationship to tradition is primal, I think, because he got to the past through art, and his passion for art and its tradition simply transferred to history as a whole. "As for me," he has said, "I want to remember *everything.* I'm not a primitive or a space cadet." ("Space cadet" is the epithet Levine began using around 1950 to refer to avant-gardists, especially the Abstract Expressionists.) For him history is all of the past, but especially the history of art, beginning with the litany of names (above all, Rembrandt, Titian, Rubens, Goya, Velázquez, El Greco—his favorites),

STRING QUARTET 1934–37
(Illustrated in color on page 25, with commentary by Jack Levine)

and on to the glory of their deeds and the mystery of their magical skills: the priceless heritage of the ages caught forever in the deathless evidence of their technique. That is his palpable tie to the gods of the past, and as he takes joy in emulating them, he pays them homage. Jack simply enjoys the act of painting, which for him is an endlessly fascinating discourse with tradition. His conversation is full of references to the great painters of the past, and his canvases are rich with cherished quotations of color, texture, luminosity, brushwork, scrumbling, and palette-knife swagger, recalling the sensuosity of the Venetians, the iridescence of Rubens, the lush impasto of Rembrandt, or the cool perfection of Velázquez.

The scope of Social Realism was quite broad in subject as well as style. On the whole the tendency was to deal seriously with fundamental problems of contemporary society in crisis, i.e., class struggle, war, strikes, riots, lynchings, injustice, exploitation, unemployment, poverty, hunger, etc. These were treated dramatically, tragically, sentimentally, objectively, or in any other appropriately compelling manner that could move an audience. Among the traditional rhetorical devices in the arts, satire has had a long and effective history as a critical instrument in revealing social evil and human frailty, and it found its proponents among the Social Realists. Levine belongs to a lineage that goes back, in most recent times, to Hogarth, Goya, and Daumier, and to George Grosz, one of the few 20th-century artists whom Jack admits to respecting. Satire can be a more effective instrument of propaganda than rational exposition; thus the importance of the cartoon in journalism, and the disparagement of satirical art as cartooning and propaganda. As a painter, Jack has a long list of heroes, among whom are a special pantheon of names; but as a satirist, there are only a chosen few: Goya, Daumier, Nast, and Grosz.

Satire depends on the cutting edge of wit rather than the reassuring balm of humor. In his art, his writing, and his talk, Jack Levine's style is unquestionably witty. He never puns or tells funny stories. His satire is not like the black, coruscating nightmares of Goya or the bitter invective of Grosz; it is closer to the ridicule of Daumier. Jack's wit, like Daumier's, is humane, even at its most pointed. He has even expressed an ambiguity of feeling toward protagonists in his paintings, although he seems generally to make his opinions fairly apparent. It is true that there is an underlying concern in his art with the injustices of life and society, with good and evil, and with moral rectitude, but what comes through most clearly are the incongruous relationships, ludicrous events, and ironies of existence that somehow define our political, social, and cultural character. Jack's painting is his private *comédie humaine*. His rogues' gallery, by his own admission, comes from old Hollywood gangster films, and in this he is again, in his own eccentric way, completely American. Our morals, ethics, mythology, and dreams come prepackaged, immediately usable and equally disposable, from our movies or television, depending on one's age.

There is, however, one aspect of Jack's cultural profile that strikes me as strange—his passion for *The Threepenny Opera*, which I happen to share. Given Bertholt Brecht's 1920s postwar German bitter decadence, it would hardly seem an American ideal. However, Brecht was no ordinary decadent but a radical positivist whose stock-in-trade was irony. Add that the *Dreigroschenoper* was based on John Gay's 18th-century English ballad-opera, *The Beggars' Opera*; that Kurt Weill, Brecht's musical collaborator, was not only a brilliant avant-garde composer but a writer of nostalgic lyrical melodies; and that Brecht and Weill, like much of Europe, were then enamored of American popular culture, and the conjunction becomes more comprehensible. *The Threepenny Opera* can serve Jack as a paradigm because it is a radical utopian tract masquerading as a picaresque fable. In it, good and evil are interchangeable; nothing can be trusted to be what it should; sophistication is the ultimate innocence, as exemplified by Jenny, the golden-hearted prostitute, the ultimate cliché; and Queen Victoria supplies a happy ending. But there is ample opportunity in the

GANGSTER FUNERAL 1952–53
(Illustrated in color on page 60, with commentary by Jack Levine on page 59)

THE SYNDICATE, 1939
(Illustrated in color on page 32, with commentary by Jack Levine)

interstices of the plot to lampoon all the injustices of society and the foibles of people. The barbs aimed at capitalism, male exploitation of women, and crime and venality as the currency of existence are done with a light-hearted insouciance sharpened by an underlying ironic bite. The Marc Blitzstein adaptation may have blunted the original, especially in the transformation of this bitter decadence, but then Jack also lacks the ultimate pessimism of Middle Europe.

I am also fascinated by Jack's assessment of America's most famous popular artist, Norman Rockwell. Against all accepted aesthetic dogma, Jack not only admires his skill but recognizes his art from a critical point of view by comparing his own pessimistic view of America with Rockwell's optimistic one. Jack is obviously worried about his own negativism. "One fears to be a Norman Rockwell. However, I think we'll find that Norman Rockwell was a critic too. [His art] is going to amount to a vast, many-sided statement about platitudes in America, if *only* that. For my part, I think it's safer to be negative, especially in the 20th century. There's plenty to be negative about, except that in the long run it's the same thing. It depends on your personality." In the end, the art will remain, whether couched in positive or negative terms. Jack sees Rockwell's art as a comment on American life, which with all its positivism will remain a critique of bourgeois culture in 20th-century America. Actually, Rockwell's encyclopedic catalogue of bourgeois moral, ethical, social, and cultural values is so accurate in its own terms that it will eventually be seen for what it is—a benign satire. In the end, Rockwell's art will remain a remarkable record of American life seen in terms of all the accepted clichés we have lived by, the mythology we believed in. Some day, perhaps, Rockwell's America will seem a "true" picture, at least truer than Andrew Wyeth's poetic fantasy, and I mean in aesthetic terms as well. When Jack says, "in the long run it's the same thing," he recognizes that ultimately the positive or negative stance will become irrelevant; it is the artistic statement that will count.

Unlike Rockwell, Jack's cultural stance was colored by the Depression, as well as by his ethnic, economic, social, and cultural background. He grew up a poor, first-generation Jew in Boston, with an early-discovered talent and passion for art. The culture he soon moved into, unlike that of his immediate family, was bohemian, perhaps somewhat less so in Boston than in New York. The economic, political, and cultural attitudes of intellectuals and artists were generally left-leaning, in a spread from reform to revolution, from the New Deal to Communism, searching for immediate panaceas to promised utopias. Few artists were Republicans. The artist, like anyone else, faced the threat of unemployment and hunger, and, toward the end of the '30s, imminent war and, especially for Jews, the specter of Fascism. Even as a young man, from the very beginning, Jack's art was fraught with angst. It was quite logical for him to look for artistic models among the Middle European Expressionists such as Soutine, Beckmann, and Kokoschka rather than the School of Paris.

I first met Jack in 1938 when I came to Harvard as a graduate student in art history. I knew Jack's work and went to visit his studio with a fellow student from Boston who had already met him. I got to know Jack better after the war when he came to live in New York. We had a great deal in common, including similar ethnic backgrounds and a passion for art and baseball. Over the years we have found grounds for agreement about many things, but we have some real difficulties about art and baseball. Artists, by vocation, tend to be self-involved, and their views on art are limited by their own interests and are fairly intense. Art historians, on the other hand, by the very nature of their vocation, have a more catholic view of art, even though they also have particular preferences. To artists, art historians must seem equivocal, uncommitted, too evenhanded. To art historians, most artists seem prejudiced, narrow-minded, and intolerant. As a result there is a lot of opportunity for argument and misunderstanding. But we have learned to become a bit more tolerant of each other, or at least to avoid the by now obvious confrontations. In baseball Jack and I do not have the natural antipathy we have in art, since we are both fans, but we do have different and irreconcilable loyalties. Coming from Boston, Jack is naturally a dyed-in-the-wool Red Sox fan, and coming from Brooklyn, I was originally a Dodgers fan, but, due to circumstances I shall try to explain, became a Yankees rooter. The Yankees and the Red Sox are eternal rivals, a condition that dates back to the '20s when the Red Sox, for no explainable reason except filthy lucre, sold their star pitcher and batter, the immortal Babe Ruth, to the Yankees. It was a complete and heartless sellout and betrayal, for which the Red Sox fans have never forgiven the Red Sox management or the Yankees. The Red Sox fans' loyalty is therefore legendary and limited—passionately devoted to the players and the team, and totally suspicious of management, while nursing an undying hatred of the Yankees, who, since the days of the Babe, have won more consistently than anyone else. This of course has rankled in every loyal Bostonian's breast for more than half a century. The frustration and rage continues. In addition, Jack and I had our individual heroes who embodied this rivalry on an unparalled level of greatness—Ted Williams of the Red Sox and Joe DiMaggio of the Yankees. Which was greater? We still debate that historic confrontation with undiminished partisanship and unchanging argument. They remain for us metaphors of artistry on the purest level, without politics or prejudice, just as baseball, the incomparable sport, is a metaphor for art, beauty, and truth.

I was a Brooklyn Dodgers fan at a time when they habitually and ineptly ended the season in last place or reasonably close to it. At the age of about 12, despite the ritual off-season exercise in proving that the Dodgers were man-for-man the best team in the league and "wait until next year," I could no longer suffer the situation and, out-facing the censure of my peers, switched my allegiance to the Yankees. (No Brooklyn fan ever defected to the Giants.) I now recognize that act as possibly reflecting a basic weakness in my moral fiber, but the pragmatism has made my life much more pleasant. As a matter of fact, when Jack moved to New York, I suggested that he might put all those years of frustration behind him and become a Yankees fan. No way. I decided that Bostonians must get used to frustration and probably consider it, like heartburn, a normal condition of life. In the last few years, as the Yankees have faltered, the Red Sox have had a real resurgence with great pitching, terrific hitting, and fine fielding, and then the Wade Boggs scandal struck. Jack took it with Job-like stoicism. "There we go again," is all he said. Jack remains loyal, just as he does in his art. And I must say I admire him for it.

Recently, Jack has commented, "Looking back on the '70s, it seems to me as if that political motivation—that desire to satirize, to tweak the noses of the powers that be—had died in me. But when I actually look at the work I did then, I realize that I was doing as much painting of that kind as I had ever done, even though other artists I knew were not bothering with it anymore. I was alone at the old stand."

Biographical Outline

Compiled by Susanna Levine Fisher

1915
Born January 3 in Boston, Mass., of Lithuanian Jewish parents.

1924–31
Studies drawing with Harold K. Zimmerman at Community Center, Roxbury, Mass.

1929–33
Studies painting under tutelage of Dr. Denman W. Ross, Department of Art, Harvard University, Cambridge, Mass., with fellow student Hyman Bloom.

1932
Drawings included in a show at Fogg Art Museum, Harvard, organized by Dr. Ross.

1935
Twenty of Levine's drawings bequeathed by Dr. Ross to Fogg Art Museum. Others subsequently given by Prof. Paul. J. Sachs.

1935–40
Employed intermittently as an artist by the Easel Division of the WPA Federal Art Project, Boston.

1936
Exhibits paintings for the first time in New York City, at the Museum of Modern Art (*Card Game* and *Brain Trust*).

1937
First included in Whitney Museum of American Art's Annual Exhibition (*String Quartet*). *The Feast of Pure Reason* placed on indefinite loan to the Museum of Modern Art. First exhibition at the Downtown Gallery. Released from the WPA Federal Art Project.

1938
Readmitted to the WPA Federal Art Project. *The Feast of Pure Reason* exhibited at Musée du Jeu de Paume, Paris. First included in Carnegie Institute's International Exhibition, Pittsburgh, Pa.

1939
First solo exhibition, at the Downtown Gallery. *Nighttown Scene* exhibited at New York World's Fair, then purchased and presented to Addison Gallery of American Art, Andover, Mass. His father dies.

1940
For the last time, dropped from the WPA Federal Art Project. First included in Annual Exhibition of the Pennsylvania Academy of the Fine Arts, Philadelphia, Pa. (*Street Scene No. 2*).

1942–45
Drafted into U.S. Army; serves in the U.S. and on Ascension Island, in the South Atlantic; discharged as technical sergeant in 1945.

1942
String Quartet purchased by the Metropolitan Museum of Art, New York, for its permanent collection after including it in *Artists for Victory* exhibition and awarding it Second Purchase Prize. Reproductions of *String Quartet* displayed in New York City subway cars.

1943
First included in the Biennial Exhibition of the Corcoran Gallery of Art, Washington, D.C.

1945
Receives John Simon Guggenheim Memorial Fellowship (May 1945–May 1946). *The Syndicate* purchased for the Encyclopaedia Brittanica Collection, Chicago, Ill.; *Neighborhood Physician* purchased by Walker Art Center, Minneapolis, Minn.

1946
Marries painter Ruth Gikow. Moves to New York, to 97 St. Mark's Place. Awarded second prize by Carnegie Institute, Pittsburgh, for *Welcome Home*; receives Grant Award from National Institute of Arts and Letters, New York. Guggenheim Fellowship renewed for one year (May 1946–May 1947).

1947
Travels and studies in Europe with Ruth Gikow. Awarded third prize and bronze medal by the Corcoran Gallery of Art, Washington, D.C., for *Apteka*. First included in an exhibition at the Brooklyn Museum; included in a traveling exhibition in Europe organized by the U.S. Department of State.

1948
Awarded Jennie Sesnan Gold Medal by Pennsylvania Academy of the Fine Arts for *Apteka*. Chosen by *Look* Magazine as one of "Ten Best American Painters."

1949
The Downtown Gallery publishes his print *Hebrew King*. Daughter, Susanna, born.

1950
Teaches advanced painting at Cleveland Institute of Art, Cleveland, Ohio.

1950–51
Receives Fulbright grant for one year's study in Rome.

1951
Included in *I São Paulo Bienal*, Brazil.

1952–55
First retrospective exhibition of his work is organized, at the Institute of Contemporary Art, Boston, and travels to museums in five other U.S. cities (including the Phillips Collection, Washington, D.C., in 1953, and the Whitney Museum of American Art, New York, in 1955).

1953
Exhibition of paintings and drawings at the Alan Gallery, New York.

1953–54
Teaches summer school at Skowhegan School of Painting and Sculpture, Skowhegan, Maine.

1955
Elected as a member of the American Academy of Arts and Sciences, Boston.

1956
Included in *XXVIII Venice Biennale*, Italy. Elected as a member of the National Institute of Arts and Letters, New York.

1957
Included in the *First Annual Guggenheim International Award Exhibition*, Solomon R. Guggenheim Museum, New York. Awarded Honorary Doctor of Fine Arts degree, Colby College, Waterville, Maine.

1958
Awarded Grand Painting Prize, Instituto Nacional de Bellas Artes, Mexico City. Teaches painting at Philadelphia Museum of Fine Arts. New York Graphic Society publishes *Teachers and Kings* (facsimile reproductions of six portrait paintings of biblical characters).

1959
Welcome Home shown in Moscow. Travels in Europe with his wife and daughter. Awarded Second W. A. Clark Prize by the Corcoran Gallery of Art, Washington, D.C., for *The Girls from Fleugel Street*. His mother dies.

1960
Thirty paintings featured in a Sala de Honor of *Il Bienal Interamericana*, Instituto Nacional de Bellas Artes, Mexico City.

1962
Elected as a member of the Board of Governors, Skowhegan School of Painting and Sculpture; resigns within the year. Visits Israel for the first time.

1964
Awarded Walter Lippincott Prize by the Pennsylvania Academy of the Fine Arts for *The Last Waltz*.

1966
Jack Levine published by Harry N. Abrams, Inc.

1966–69
Teaches painting at the Pennsylvania Academy of the Fine Arts.

1967
The Dreigroschenfilm (The Threepenny Film, a suite of 20 soft-ground etchings) published.

1968
Retrospective exhibition at the DeCordova Museum, Lincoln, Mass.

1970
Facing East (a limited-edition portfolio of lithographs, woodcuts, and pochoir-and-phototype reproductions) is published, with an introduction by James Michener.

1972
First exhibition at Kennedy Galleries, New York. Travels to Israel and Spain with Ruth.

1973
Elected as a member of the American Academy of Arts and Letters, New York. *Cain and Abel* acquired by the Vatican Museums for their permanent collection.

1975
Awarded Altman Prize by the National Academy of Design, New York, for *The Perpetrator*.

1977
Included in a traveling exhibition in the USSR, organized by the Metropolitan Museum of Art, New York, and the Fine Arts Museums of San Francisco.

1978–80
Retrospective exhibition is organized at the Jewish Museum, New York, and travels to five other U.S. cities.

1982
Ruth Gikow dies on April 2. He travels to Rome, Israel, and Greece with daughter, Susanna.

1984
The Complete Graphic Work of Jack Levine published by Dover Press.

1985
Jack Levine: Feast of Pure Reason, a David Sutherland film, is produced; it premieres in 1986 at the Museum of Fine Arts, Boston, the Museum of Modern Art, New York, and the National Gallery of Art, Washington, D.C. He gives advanced summer painting class at University of Haifa, Israel.

1986
Quits Kennedy Galleries.

JACK LEVINE

ON

JACK LEVINE

EDITOR'S NOTE: Jack Levine's commentaries on his life and work have been compiled from a variety of sources, primarily recorded interviews that have been transcribed and edited, and sometimes from essays and statements that he has occasionally written over the years. Attributions of the source(s) for each commentary are provided on page 140, along with a more complete explanation.

The Early Years

I was born January 3, 1915 in the South End of Boston about two blocks away from Dover Street, just off Harrison Avenue in what they called the New York streets. Dover Street was a skid row; I think it still is. The area was teeming, full of pawnshops. It was very like Hester Street in New York in the old days. But everything changes. I loved the action there even when I was a little boy. I loved the drunks. I loved the cops. I loved the pushcarts and the horse-drawn wagons. I loved the ladies with mens' caps pushing vegetables and fruit and what-not. And years later, I began to draw the things that I loved most and remembered best. This was imbued in me. I used to dream about it.

My mother always let me keep my pencils, crayons and papers in the oven of the coal stove in the kitchen during the hot summer months while she cooked on the gas range. Then when the weather grew cold, I was moved to the ice-box. Milk and other spoilables were then kept outside on the window ledge and the stove came into play. As summer came on again, I was shifted again. And so my mother and I dodged each other in her kitchen, and so the seasons passed.

She always reminisced about my early efforts to draw an automobile. She said I always put the driver in the back. I submit I was drawing a hook-and-ladder firetruck and that I was putting the rear steersman where he belonged.

It was not so long after World War I. I have faint memories of the Great Boston Police Strike with the helmeted, bayonetted National Guard at every corner of the Washington–Dover Street intersection under the El. I would go to the shoe store on Harrison Avenue where my sister worked, and there on sheets of wrapping paper do drawings of the soldiers, taking pains with the detail of their wraparound leggings and cartridge pockets.

In school we were issued shiny brass cups and hard oblongs of Milton Bradley watercolor. We were told not to use a pencil but to begin with color. On an orangey, still watery tone I would set in the features of one of those epic child-hood prototypes—jack-o-lantern, snowman, Raggedy Anne—watching the watery paper pull the features into radiating threads, blotting, puddling, striating, so that to my delight the expression of the face would change, now winking, now smirking wonderfully. I am not over the thrill of it yet.

But when the teacher said we were to do designs in axial balance or central balance, I would become a class problem.

I would go upstairs to draw with the Rosato boys. We would sit around and draw and crayon land and sea battles. I remember an argument as to whether the sea should be colored blue or green. I voted for green, having seen the water in the channel between the South End and South Boston. Over us hung a large framed photograph of St. Peter's in Rome, which I thought to be the National Capitol. We would write away for free brochures on mail-order courses in cartooning. One of them—was it the Washington or the Landon School of Cartooning?—had as a frontispiece a photo of the school's president, who was George Luks!

It may have been my third-grade teacher who arranged for me to go to the South Bay Union. A neighborhood facility, it was run, I believe, by the Cathedral of the Holy Cross. I suppose it was denominational enough, but I saw no overt sign of it. Rather there was an abundance of geometric wooden shapes—cones, cubes, cylinders, prisms—which we were to do in light and shade with charcoal. I was given charcoal, an enormous white sheet of paper and, I think, a pyramid to interpret. Near me a big boy buzzed like a summer fly and drummed his fingers. With this music in my ears I wrestled with the third dimension.

The instructor came in and busied himself copying what I later knew to be one of Sir Joshua Reynolds' angels from a sepia Perry Print. Later he looked at what I was doing. He didn't seem to see any talent in it. After he went back to his angel I turned the sheet over and drew with the charcoal something more to my liking—a huge battleship, her funnels belching charcoal smoke, all guns firing. When I got home, I told my mother they had tried to make me draw a cross.

Before I entered the fifth grade, we moved to Roxbury. I was sent to the children's Saturday morning classes at the Boston Museum. I was vaguely familar with the Museum, having been brought to admire the Atheneum portrait of George Washington by Gilbert Stuart.

I was set to copying a Japanese gazelle in the act of springing violently in opposite directions. I had a watercolor block and a box of colors. The first objective was to lay a smooth wash—a mixture of raw sienna with perhaps a dab of black and earth red to simulate the raw silk basis on which the original was done. I never did succeed in laying that even wash. I don't remember getting to the next stage. I believe I was in that class for two years, and to this day I doubt I can lay an even watercolor wash.

A friend took me to a settlement house in Roxbury, where, to my concern, I was to be taken into a class which consisted of making beautiful patterns of Hebrew letters in whole or in part—doubled, tripled, quadrupled, upside down or backwards, the final design done in Mughal colors. Presiding over the class was a rabbinical candidate with his mind on other matters.

Fortunately, it turned out that a new class was opening. We met with the new teacher, a student of the Museum School, with narrow eyes, bushy auburn hair and the moustache which is the insignia of our profession. This was Harold Zimmerman, my new teacher. I demanded, "Are you going to make us copy and do designs?" He said we could draw whatever we liked. Zimmerman was nine years older than I. He was trying to make a living as an art teacher. He taught art in several settlement houses around Boston. While I was studying with him in

THE ORGAN GRINDER 1931
Graphite on tan paper, 11 x 15 in.
Fogg Art Museum, Harvard University
Cambridge, Mass.
Anonymous Gift

Roxbury, Hyman Bloom was studying with him in a settlement house in Boston's West End. Zimmerman was my teacher for about seven years. I met him when I was about nine years old and we parted company when I was about 16.

Zimmerman kept us working practically all day during the summer months, especially after he had his own art school, which was subsidized by Dr. Denman W. Ross. Under Zimmerman, we followed what you would call imaginative drawing, never based on the use of a model. We developed our own art vocabulary from observation and from study of what the great artists of the past had done, using what was needed from everything we saw and remembered. In his method of teaching, the idea was to take it in and remember. If you don't remember, you go back or go see a piece of sculpture or some old master's drawings, but most often I would go back and look. Zimmerman taught drawing from the Alberti viewpoint. This is the knowledge of natural and scientific laws governing appearances; compositional drawing; and an essentially analytical approach.

Working from Greek casts, I couldn't draw accurately until my knowledge of the human figure reached a parallel point—apparently that's what Zimmerman intended in his teaching method. You help yourself where you can—I took from all sources. It isn't just the eye—it isn't just a question of realism—it's a question of articulation about images. I had contempt for drawing from life; I thought it was copying. I formed an early hostility to copying. Zimmerman would talk about some aspect of form or line, but not much. To be sure, when I became sophisticated enough, I could and did make many portraits from life.

I studied drawing with Zimmerman and painting with Denman Ross. I met Ross when I had just turned 14. He was 77 years old when I met him; he was Professor Emeritus of Harvard. He was a theoretical Impressionist; his approach to drawing was synthetic—just the opposite to Zimmerman's. Ross thought some of Zimmerman's mannerisms in his approach to drawing were "rhetorical flourishes"—to quote him exactly. I had never painted. I could draw—he liked that. He did not have to teach me to draw a nose, for example. We would discuss the light or color intensity of the highlight on the nose and he could rely on me to put it in the right place. Ross had all kinds of theories about the palette. He put me on a salary of twelve dollars a week, and it was worth it to him. For the twelve dollars he gave me, he had the best toy he ever had. Consider it, at 14 I was a formidable draftsman, just ready to learn how to paint, and Ross had in me a perfect student to test his theories. He believed in controlling the color circle—180 degrees from hot to cold colors. I informed myself about his theories but I did not adopt them. He espoused the Impressionists' theories of light and color. I favored the old masters, but I have more respect now than ever for his science in art that seems so neglected these days. His theories of design are broad and simple—perhaps because of his deep knowledge of Oriental art—and his theories preceded as well as superseded most of the abstract theories of the School of Paris. His color theories toward the end of his life became simpler and more workable. His systematic palettes were then organized scales of color with simple principles of warm and cool contrasts. My basic departure from Ross rests in my much stronger interest in the densities of paint (underpainting, glazings, scumblings, thick-and-thin applications, etc.), all matters that Ross and the Impressionist school, for the most part, did not really face.

In 1932, when I was still in my second year of high school, I was in an exhibition at the Fogg Museum. Dr. Ross had arranged it. He bought some of my drawings and gave them to the Fogg, and Professor Paul J. Sachs bought several from this exhibition.

My training involved me in what later I decided was the Alberti ideal of the *istoria*, the historical painting, the painting that has a tableau of figures acting in a certain way, which forces you to know anatomy and perspective and all the elements of the Renaissance approach to art. And I felt that I needed subject matter. I needed it in the sense that I felt that I was moving in some sort of drama in the tableau. And it seemed to me before I was interested in any political issues

STUDY OF HAROLD ZIMMERMAN ca. 1931
Graphite on light green paper, 15 x 11 in.
Fogg Art Museum, Harvard Universtiy, Cambridge, Mass.
Anonymous gift

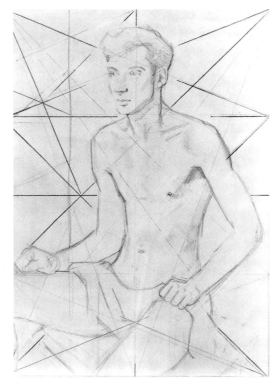

SEATED NUDE YOUTH 1933
Graphite on olive brown paper, 14 x 10 in.
Fogg Art Museum, Harvard University
Cambridge, Mass.
Bequest of Dr. Denman W. Ross, 1975

at all that the few cartoons that I saw of the Left, such as in the *New Masses*, looked like very good dramatic material. At the time I had these considerations I might have been 17 or 18 years old. And I had some friends with similar interests. I think perhaps about that time I saw Grosz's drawing of Jesus Christ on the Cross with a gas mask and jack boots. It seemed like there was an epic about to unfold about the whole Passion of the working class. That's the way I was going.

And most important, two things: When I was 13, I saw the opera *Boris Godunov*, which was a tremendous emotional experience and I think showed me the way I wanted to go, like a headlight down the track. And the other thing was Pabst's film of *The Threepenny Opera*, by Bertolt Brecht and Kurt Weill, which I saw with a friend by playing hooky from school and going to the Fine Arts Theater on Norway Street, in Boston's Back Bay. And that made me one of the first native Brechtians in America. *The Threepenny Opera* was a kind of great motivating idea of art and politics. I think I learned more from that film than almost anything else, although it was in German and I hardly understood a word, but I seemed to think that I knew that I ought to go that way—in other words, not in the direction of the epic Mexican frescoes, not in the direction of the political cartooning that was going on, but in some sense that this film showed me. It gave me a kind of working morale and a sense of subject, a certain outlook on the world. There is a touch of nostalgia that the film had too.

PORTRAIT OF KANJI NAKAMURA 1931
Graphite on white paper, 15 x 11¾ in.
Fogg Art Museum, Harvard University, Cambridge, Mass.
Anonymous gift

I saw these things through a lens of my own poverty. I was very embittered and I had every reason to be. In the early 1930s I had nothing at all. And then providentially, when things were just so bad they couldn't get any worse, the WPA came along—or at any rate I got on it. And, while I am of two minds about government intervention in the arts, sometimes I think that there are frightening possibilities. I still think so. At that time it was one of the best things that ever happened to me in my life. For the first time in my life I was a part of some sort of organization of artists. What we had in Massachusetts was the Artists and Writers Union. I began to go to the meetings.

I began to hand out leaflets. I went up and down Washington Street in what they called the "borax furniture stores" getting people to sign petitions to keep the project alive. You see, it was a fight always between the left and the right. And the right was trying to destroy the projects. They didn't like the idea at all of any money passing to people except through their hands. At any rate, I found myself with petitions. I found myself with leaflets. And I was very busy. As I recall, I only did one thing as an artist for all of this. I did a cover for an Artists and Writers Union bulletin of Uncle Sam being pleaded with by a little boy artist and a little girl artist with Uncle Sam striding between them indifferently. I like that kind of negative thing.

When I was twenty, I hung out with some young WPA artists in Boston's Back Bay. One evening one of them suggested that we all go over to the Copley Society and sketch from life. Well, I never had, but I could draw as well as any of them, so I went with them. When the model came out dressed in a robe and then took it off, I went into shock. I had never seen a nude woman before in my life. And I thought what I saw was just great. I do not know what kind of drawing I did. I think, maybe, that I just looked at her and did not pay much attention to what I was drawing. But I do remember thinking this is a great reason to be an artist. I thought about my misspent youth and the drawing and painting I had done from the Parker boys in Denman Ross's studio, and I looked at this terrific girl and felt like a refugee from the YMCA. This a landmark in my life.

There I was in Boston, and everybody in Boston said you have to go to New York, there's nothing here. And they were mistaken, because it was much better for me to be in Boston. I was much better trained than I would have been in New York.

But by the time I was in my early twenties, I was kind of feisty, and I began to have some sense of my own power instead of being intimidated by teachers. I got very interested in Central European Expressionism—in George Grosz, Max Beckmann, and Oscar Kokoschka, who I think painted the greatest portraits of the twentieth century. Now, you couldn't find anything like that in Boston. I also must say that you couldn't find any German Expressionism in New York then, either. It was a very rare thing. You could see Braques till the cows came home. You could see anything French. But German art couldn't get past that French curtain. This was possibly my first experience with the lines of force in the marketplace. I was really interested in this kind of art. The only thing I had to go by was one book, of which I have a copy, Carl Einstein's *The Art of the Twentieth Century*—and the twentieth century has gone a long way since then. But this had Rouault, Kokoschka, Picasso, Chagall, and so on. It had all the contemporary artists that you could see in New York, and other things that had never reached New York, and God help us in Boston. Hyman Bloom and I were mad about Soutine. If we got wind of a big show of Soutine in New York, we were not to be seen in Boston. Forget it. We'd be off on the night bus.

I took my place in the late 1930s in the great uprising of social consciousness that was going on in the United States and all over the world. Generally speaking, around me, artists were influenced by and involved with the Mexican fresco movement and a certain amount of Cézannishness and Cubism. And, of course, there was the regional school that was painting some sort of drama of America. I, for my part, remained deeply committed to the physiognomy and psychology of man. And I found that the painting of Middle Europe was especially moving and sympathetic to me. The work of Grosz, Beckmann, and Kokoschka and the writings of Brecht—I found these very eloquent and meaningful.

Most artists in the '30s, however, did not paint the social situation that was evident all around them; they painted their own crises. But they had some sort of naive hope that the renaissance was coming, that their painting was leading toward a revolution that would solve everything. I didn't paint these things to reach an audience, because I was never sure that I'd reach anyone. I never have the sense that an editor has of a readership, or that a politician has of a constituency. I started out as a serious, hard-working painter, but I knew damn well that paintings of mine, if they got to museums, wouldn't have any social effect. I think I painted them just to paint them, and to express myself, because I believe that political expression in painting is a kind of self-expression. If that's the way your mind runs at a certain time, it would be repressive and self-defeating to muzzle it. Social expression in art is like writing a letter to your congressman, or writing an article for a newspaper. It is part of being a citizen, and it can express itself in anything—painting, too. I never made any requirement, though perhaps some people did, that a painter should be a political painter. You should paint nudes, if that's what grabs you; it grabs me sometimes. Whatever it is that's on your mind should find an outlet.

For me, the '30s was a very productive period. I not only got 23 dollars a week, but the WPA also had its own galleries. And national shows—that is, shows national in scope—were organized. A big WPA show was organized at the Duncan Phillips Gallery in Washington which came to the Museum of Modern Art in New York. I had some paintings in these two exhibitions and I got national publicity. And that seemed fine. But then the bottom fell out. The WPA office got word that the welfare office wanted to see me. Just a technicality. So I went over there, and I was told that I was not eligible for welfare and had to be fired from the WPA program.

By that time, I had been discovered by the Downtown Gallery, which was then perhaps the most important gallery of American art. However, I made hardly a dime during the seven years I was with them. And the Museum of Modern Art got two of my paintings from the WPA without paying me a cent—*The Street* and *The Feast of Pure Reason*. (They have a hundred-year lease on *Feast*; I think

NIGHTTOWN SCENE 1936
Oil on plywood, 48 x 24 in.
San Francisco Museum of Modern Art
WPA Federal Art Project Allocation to San Francisco Museum of Art

CARD GAME 1933
Oil on canvas, 21 x 26 in.
Collection of the artist

it says on the frame, "Property of the U.S. Government".) In 1942 the Modern was interested in buying *The Passing Scene*, and the price was $475. They offered me $250, and I declined. I wasn't going to cut my prices like that, even for them. Nothing doing. So they came up to my figure, and that's the way it wound up.

The artists who were big in the WPA have been neglected since their heyday; there seems to be a prejudice against them in Republican administrations. They've been officially cast into outer darkness because they represent a political situation that was an embarassment to the powers-that-be. The '30s were a period when the right-of-center, Republican powers-that-be couldn't cope. This was a shameful period (to them), and they would just as soon forget about it. There is an official indifference or obscurantism about the '30s. I've seen nostalgia about the '60s, but about the '30s there's practically nothing left.

In 1939 my father died. And I was very hard hit by that. And I began to paint this long series of miniatures on the kings and teachers of Israel. He was called Samuel, but his name in Hebrew would have been Solomon, or Shelomo. So the first painting I did in this series was of Solomon.

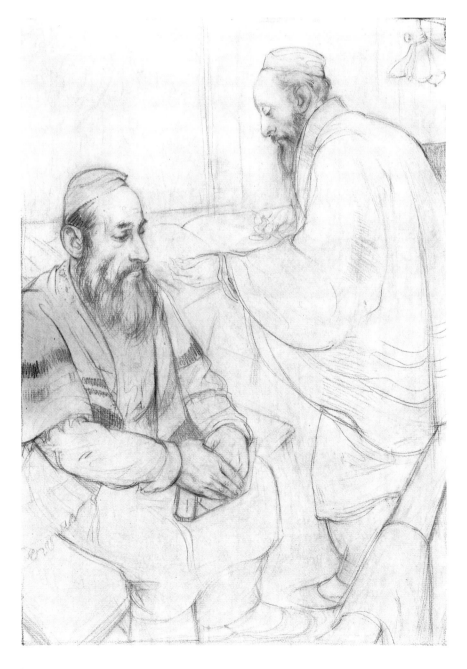

SHELOMO 1941
Oil on panel, 12 x 9 in.
Whereabouts unknown

JEWISH CANTORS IN THE SYNAGOGUE 1930
Red and black chalk on gray paper, 18¾ x 12½ in.
Fogg Art Museum, Harvard University, Cambridge, Mass.
Bequest of Dr. Denman W. Ross, 1975

BRAIN TRUST (Conference) 1935
Oil on canvas, 48 x 24 in.
Whereabouts unknown

above right:

DISCUSSION 1935
Graphite on beige paper, 10¹¹⁄₁₆ x 7⁷⁄₁₆ in.
Fogg Art Museum, Harvard University, Cambridge, Mass.
Gift of William Germain Dooley

By the time I was in my late teens I had become a highly skilled draftsman, doing representational pencil drawings of figures that were as good as anyone trained at the Slade School in London might have done. But at the age of 19 or 20, after my bitter experience with the WPA, I went through a period of self-examination and the hormonal changes of entering manhood, and I decided that I was no longer interested in elegance of style or strict verisimilitude, but something more raw and explosive. I was very much influenced by Hyman Bloom, and we had both become avid partisans of Soutine, Rouault, and (I more strongly than Bloom) Kokoschka. I began to do paintings that vehemently expressed my resentment about my place in the world. *Brain Trust,* which was also called *Conference,* draws on my experience of walking through Boston Common, whose Parkman Bandstand is pretty much equivalent to Hyde Park Corner in London or what Union Square used to be in New York—a place for impromptu soapbox speakers to rally a crowd and say what's on their minds, and for people to sit around and argue politics and religion. Parkman Bandstand also had more than a touch of Skid Row about it then. The rheumy, red-eyed man sitting against the backrest looks like a typical denizen of that part of the city, but the little fat man with the handlebar moustache and heavy gold watch chain is my own invention. Behind them is my attempt at painting the Soldiers and Sailors Monument.

THE QUARTET 1931
Graphite on pale blue-gray paper, 11¹¹⁄₁₆ x 15¹⁄₁₆ in.
Fogg Art Museum, Harvard University, Cambridge, Mass.
Bequest of Dr. Denman W. Ross, 1975

STRING QUARTET NO. 2 ca. 1939
Oil on canvas, 20 x 27 in.
Private collection

STRING QUARTET 1934–37
Tempera and oil on masonite, 48 x 67 in.
Metropolitan Museum of Art

My background was really quite classical. In my teens I was very involved with the art of men like Leonardo da Vinci, Holbein, Ingres, and, especially, Degas, so much of whose work I was able to see at the Fogg Museum over at Harvard. And you might say I had a piece of that classical tradition. In 1934, when I was nineteen, I started to do a painting called *String Quartet*, which began as a classical exercise, some sort of Venetian effort, as I recall. I was always looking for dramatic situations to paint—tableaux of people together involved in some sort of action, or a little bit of history. *String Quartet* was never what I would call socially significant, but it's a dramatic situation—the interaction of four people. I wasn't the first to discover the beauties of the interaction of four string musicians.

In 1935, after I'd completed the underpainting for *String Quartet*, I was hired by the WPA, and I had to stop working on it and put it aside or the WPA would have claimed it. But two years later I got canned by the WPA, and I took it out again and repainted it. Well, perhaps it was just glandular, but as I became a young man I began to feel my own oats, and the repainting of *String Quartet* completely changed the way it looked. It became explosive, with loud brilliant color—or so it seemed to me at the time. And there was a dialogue between the shattering of the smooth surface and a hunger for elegance and good phrasing. *String Quartet* began in a controlled kind of classicism, with muted colors, and I poured everything I'd absorbed from the Expressionists right on top of it.

Commentary on
THE STREET
STREET SCENE NO. 1
STREET SCENE NO. 2

He is something I wrote in 1939 about the paintings I had been doing:

Essentially a city dweller, I find that the aspects of man and his environment in a large city are all I need to work with. I find my approach to painting inseparable from my approach to the world. Justice is more important than good looks. The artist must sit in judgment and intelligently evaluate the case for any aspect of the world he deals with. The validity of his work will rest on the humanity of his decision. A painting is good for the very same reason that anything in this world is good.

I feel the sordid neglect of a slum section strongly enough to wish to be a steward of its contents, to enumerate its increment—newspapers, cigarette butts, torn posters, empty match cards, broken bottles, orange rinds, overflowing garbage cans, flies, boarded houses, gas lights, and so on—to present this picture in the very places where the escapist plans his flight.

It has been an idiosyncrasy of mine to argue that a man so overtaxed in working for another man that he defeats his own cause, is not his own man. This I accept for myself as the reason why, to me, the symbol of work can never express the working man. The picture I persist in painting is an evening scene, designed to catch the man *not* at work, tired and overwhelmed but still, for the time, a free man. The consciousness that may be projected by the limpidness of an eye or a gentle incertitude of gesture is as far as I go in putting my characters into action, because of some logic of the psychological approach. Movement in my canvases embraces every object as well as atmosphere. Dramatic action on the part of the characters is latent. I distort images in an attempt to weld the drama of man and his environment.

That part of my work which is satirical is based on observations gathered in countless hours, hangling around street corners and cafeterias. There I often hear from urbane and case-hardened cronies about crooked contractors, ward heelers, racketeers, minions of the law and the like. It is my privilege as an artist to put these gentlemen on trial, to give them every ingratiating characteristic they might normally have, and then present them, smiles, benevolence and all, in my own terms.

If my frosty old gentleman in evening clothes beams with his right eye and has a cold fishy stare in his left, that is not an accident. If a policeman reposefully examines a hangnail, that is not necessarily the sum total of his activity. In this case it is an enforced genre to familiarize the spectator with the officer, to point out that he, too, has his cares and woes.

The mechanism is one of playing a counter-aspect against the original thesis, leaving it up to the spectator to judge the merits of the case. My experience is that generally the thesis is readily understood. I paint the poor and the rich, in different pictures, and give them different treatment. I think this is as it should be.

THE STREET 1938
Oil on canvas, 59½ x 83 in.
Museum of Modern Art, New York
On extended loan from the United States WPA Art Program

opposite above:

STREET SCENE NO. 1 1938
Oil on canvas, 30 x 40 in.
Museum of Fine Arts, Boston
Gift of the National Council of Jewish Women,
Boston section (to the Provisional Acquisitions Gallery)

opposite below:

STREET SCENE NO. 2 1938
Oil on masonite, 30½ x 41 in.
Portland Art Museum, Oregon
Helen Thurston Ayer Fund

THE FEAST OF PURE REASON 1937
Oil on canvas, 42 x 48 in.
The Museum of Modern Art, New York
On extended loan from the United States WPA Art Program

Study for THE FEAST OF PURE REASON ca. 1937
Ink and gouache on paper, 13 x 16¼ in.
Whereabouts unknown

I did a number of paintings in which Boston figured in the 1930s. For *The Feast of Pure Reason*, I drew on experiences I had had as a Bostonian. I sort of knew what was going on in City Hall, in the State House. I also knew something about rich men by then. I knew about the police, who were, after all, the inheritors of a strike situation and were scabs as well as policemen. I was trying, in the painting, to establish a grim and threatening atmosphere, which, I, as a young man, felt was rather scarifying.

At that time, I'd been reading James Joyce's novel *Ulysses* incessantly. Stephen Daedalus seemed to be a character from South Boston. Like Mayor James Michael Curley used to say, Boston is a day nearer Europe, and really Dublin seemed very close to Boston in those days. The title of the painting comes from the nighttown scene in which Daedalus is knocked down by two constables. They knock his glasses off and he loses his stick. Leopold Bloom, who helps the young man onto his feet says, "Your stick, sir." And Stephen says, "Stick? What need have I of a stick in this feast of pure reason?"

In terms of composition, *The Feast of Pure Reason* was inspired by a group portrait by Sir Henry Raeburn.

CITY LIGHTS NO. I 1939
Oil on canvas, 17¾ x 12 in.
Midtown Galleries, New York

I was working in an explosive style by the mid '30s. Then I became interested in distortion, such as reflections from Coney Island mirrors and all kinds of astigmatic visions. I felt I was on the brink of something very important in the sense of expressing emotion by drawing the image out in what I call a taffy-pull. At the time I seemed to think it was necessary to be an experimenter. That was the wave of that time. But it seemed to me that if I distorted things as I pleased I could put anything anywhere and have it all of human tissue. That seemed to be more important to me than translating human tissue into boxes, if you know what I mean, like a Picasso portrait.

CITY LIGHTS 1940
Oil on canvas, 54 x 36 in.
Memphis Brooks Museum of Art
Gift of Edith and Milton Lowenthal

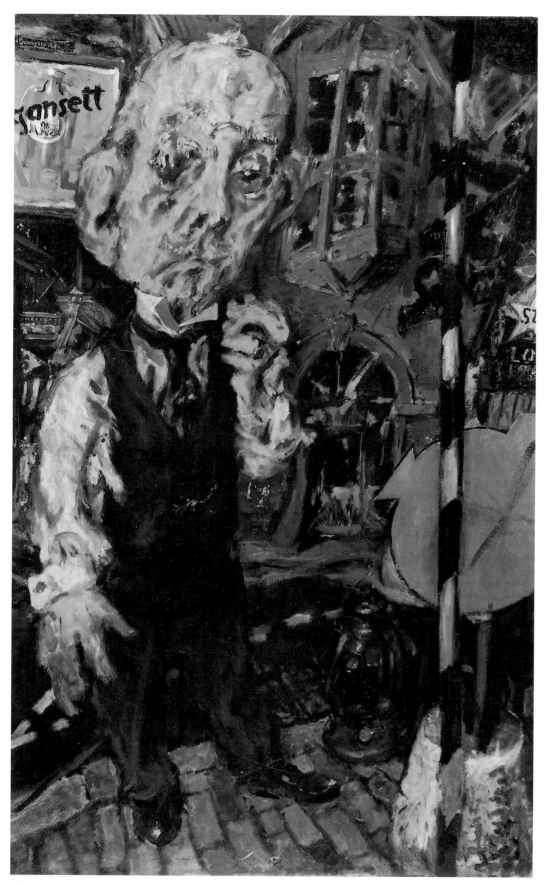

NEIGHBORHOOD PHYSICIAN 1939
Oil on composition board, 48 x 30 in.
Walker Art Center, Minneapolis
Gift of the T. B. Walker Foundation, Gilbert M. Walker Fund, 1943

Study for NEIGHBORHOOD PHYSICIAN ca. 1939
Oil on board, 12 x 8¼ in.
Whereabouts unknown

Distortion and Expressionism are not the same thing. Clouet, Corneille de Lyon distort. You distort for empathy. You give something a larger area because it is more important. And a madonna is more important than an apple, every time. You distort for editorial reasons—a dignified way of saying caricature. That has always been, and *that* isn't Expressionism. I would smooth out every brushstroke in favor of the structure of the head. I have always distorted for satire or pathos or one thing or another, but never just to express myself. Distortion is always a dramatic vehicle—drama in an external sense. The world is certain, and figures have a certain height proportionally. Sure, I distort them. It is a distortion, but it also relates.

THE SYNDICATE, 1939
Oil on canvas, 30⅛ x 45⅛ in.
Hirshhorn Museum and Sculpture Garden, Smithsonian Institution
Gift of Joseph H. Hirshhorn Foundation, 1966

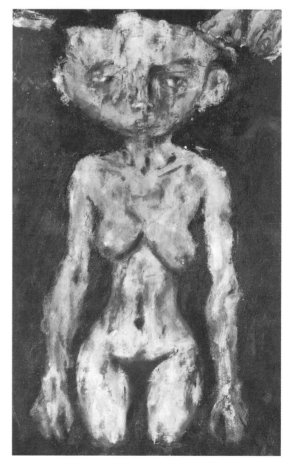

I am a physiognomist. I am convinced that there are two types of artists in this world. There is the kind that Frank Jewett Mather called "athleticists," among whom you might number Tintoretto, El Greco, Michelangelo—even Botticelli. Then there is another sort that I would characterize as interested in human psychology that is revealed by a look of an eye, a little furrow here, a mole there. And their work has its own kind of beauty. Many times I have wanted to paint a lovely girl and have her appear lovely, but it always turns out differently. She gets kind of chunky. And the rectangle gets more and more stuffed with human tissue. So, if you ever want your wife painted, do not call on me, because if one eye is a little lower than the other or she has a mole in a bad place or something like that, I will love it and I will catch it and it will be painted.

Nude, 1939–40, was an effort to do an Expressionist nude, frontal. And that's all it was. It's done in wildly broken color. And it's more of a painting performance and a manipulation of oil and tempera together.

The Syndicate was an effort to paint *The Feast of Pure Reason* over again with some of the kind of distortion I began doing in the late '30s. The man on the left—the one I thought of as a rat-faced man with a long rodent-like nose and beady eyes—he was like a little gangster in the movies.

NUDE (Burlesque Dancer) ca. 1939–40
Oil on canvas, 18 x 11⅞ in.
Hirshhorn Museum and Sculpture Garden, Smithsonian Institution
Gift of Joseph H. Hirshhorn, 1966

RICH MAN, POOR MAN ca. 1940
Oil on canvas, 21 x 15 in.
Whereabouts unknown

I had become a devotee of the composer Mussorgsky after hearing his opera *Boris Godunov* when I was a teenager. *Rich Man, Poor Man* was inspired by the "Samuel Goldenberg and Schmuyle" tableau of Mussorgsky's *Pictures at an Exhibition*, which I found very amusing and which seemed to be grist for my mill. The two characters are a rich Jew and a poor Jew; the poor Jew quavers while the rich Jew walks past in a fur-collared coat and with a ponderous tread. Looking at the painting now, I see these as racist clichés, which Mussorgsky was helping to perpetuate (and not all that innocently, either). In terms of style, I was at the peak of my period of distorting, elongating, and compacting figures, and was using these techniques here to satirize the two characters: a pompous, self-important bourgeois and a pathetic little man possibly right out of Soutine. I used a strident pink heightened with blue for the poor man's flesh tones, which strongly recalls the dark pink and blue tonalities of *The Syndicate*. The two paintings are also related in theme, each showing a different aspect of the economic oppression of the poor by the rich. *The Syndicate* is my commentary on the corrupt men who run most city governments, while *Rich Man, Poor Man* takes it down to the level of the citizenry. I suppose I was making common cause with the poor man, which is a sentimental attitude, and giving voice to my feeling that no rich man deserved my sympathy. It's a rather simplistic view, but it was in the air at the time. I believed that economic determinism explained everything, and it damn near did.

The '40s

I divide the '40s, as most people would, into pre-war and post-war. My pre-war paintings were for the most part a continuation of what I'd established for myself during the '30s in terms of style and subject matter. At the beginning of the '30s I was fifteen, and my background was really quite classical. I was still trying to paint according to some kind of realistic precepts, with a certain Cézannishness coming in, although I certainly wasn't dealing with Cézanne's approach to painting. A youthful kind of drama calmly expressed became more exacerbated and a frenzy set in.

And of course the war seemed to me a little bit apocalyptic—to put it mildly. Who had any prophecy, you know? My father was probably better equipped to understand the situation in Europe at the time than I was. He came from the old country—from Lithuania, in 1898, I think, from some small village, and he probably had a better feel for this than I ever did in Boston. But he died in 1939. Although I started with his religion, it went completely counter to my social and political beliefs. At a certain point, I just absolutely refused to play that game. My father wanted me to go to Hebrew school, and I went for a while, but it backfired in *every* direction. And I quit before my thirteenth birthday. I never had a Bar Mitzvah, and he was unhappy. And yet when he died, all these brothers of mine, who went along and never questioned anything, were quite incapable of saying the Kaddish. I was the only one who could do it—I, the atheist, went through the eleven months. My mother wanted me to. You know, it was not a time when you argue atheism with your mother. So I went along, and I ended up picking up a little familiarity with the Hebrew language.

In 1942, I went into the army. First I was stationed at a base on Long Island, not far from New York City; after less than a year I was sent overseas to Ascension Island, a desert island in the South Atlantic. I'm fond of saying that if I had been a military hero, I'd really be unbearable today. But I didn't see any fighting, although there was always the possibility. I was in a troop ship for fifty-six days, and there were some subs. Ascension Island was a small base in the middle of the ocean, and it didn't have much firepower, and one of those German subs could have beat the hell out of it. But they wouldn't want to give away their position.

I did very little painting in the service. My assignment to Ascension Island was ostensibly for a project as an artist-correspondent, but nothing much came of it after I got there. What happened was that the artist George Biddle, who was the brother of the Secretary of the Navy, was determined that artists had a contribution to make. I didn't want to be an army artist. I didn't feel that the artists had a contribution to make. I remember that saying, "When the cannons roar, the muses are silent." But nobody asked me; I was a private. The commanding general of the U.S. Engineering Corps, Major General Eugene Rayburn, went before Congress to explain this project. It was a very small part of a total proposal he was making. Congress gave him a keelhauling so that you couldn't mention the project to him again. It was canceled. Now, if I had happened to be a court painter to someone like General MacArthur, I would have been allowed to work. But in the section I was in, the commanding officer was a lousy chicken colonel. He didn't have the clout to keep an artist. So I tried to keep busy. I'd been made a technical sergeant and I did a variety of jobs at the air base there—corrected the broadcasts that came in over the radio, organized a library, helped publish the camp newspaper, among other things.

After the war, I was sent to a rest camp in Virginia and then a second rest camp in North Carolina. I was on a recuperative furlough and tried to find a job in New York. I got out of the army gradually. I got a job in the army's public relations office on Lower Broadway. The PRO wanted pictures of Ascension Island, which had been a secret air base, but when the war was over they wanted to publicize it. So I wound up working in an office in New York, still in uniform. What I wanted

to do was take up my career again and come back to Boston and possibly take the studio I had. But I married Ruth Gikow in 1946 and stayed in New York. At the time, I didn't really want to get married and settle down—I had other ideas. But I let go of some of these because I know I would have given up and been back in New York in a week. It was the first time in my life that I had a few bucks. So I could afford to get married. There was army pay, and I received a Guggenheim fellowship in 1945 (plus a one-year renewal of it the following year). And I got a grant from Arts and Letters, which I think was two thousand dollars. Not only that, but the Downtown Gallery sold a lot of my paintings during the three and a half years I was in the service. And there was also the purchase prize from *String Quartet*, which the Metropolitan Museum had acquired about six or seven months after I'd begun my military service.

When I arrived in New York, I was just 30, I had had a hitch in the army, and I had a painting in the Metropolitan Museum. It isn't everyone that comes to New York that can say that. But I was singularly ill-equipped to join some other comet's tail, and consequently I set up for myself. I gave a wide berth to all the artistic cults. But I was not isolated from other artists. Ben Shahn, Jake Lawrence, and I were part of the Downtown Gallery group. We were the three political artists of that gallery. There were others like Stuart Davis, Kuniyoshi, and Charles Sheeler, too. But somebody like Shahn was of a different generation. We were never that close, and we never visited him at his farm in New Jersey. He and I really only saw each other at the gallery. There were some younger artists like Mitchell Siporin and David Fredenthal. We would have dinner parties in each other's houses, and we were close in that sense. And the Soyer brothers were like family to me.

Ruth and I went off to Europe for the first time in 1947. I had been anxious since I was very young to go to Europe and to see these things for myself instead of from reproductions. Apparently during the time I was in the army I had decided that I was going to try to master my own métier, my own materials, and to always go directly to the source. If Cézanne could go to Poussin, and Matisse could go to Cézanne and Poussin, I thought I could go to Poussin too, and even to others that I preferred to Poussin—Rembrandt, Rubens, Titian. As Matisse said, an artist should not be overly influenced by his contemporaries.

THE BANQUET 1941
Oil on canvas, 25¼ x 30 in.
Neuberger Museum, State University
of New York at Purchase
Gift of Roy R. Neuberger

Banquet began as a doodle. I had done a drawing for my own amusement, of a young fat-faced politician addressing these very shrewd old men at a political banquet, with a dream of the Capitol building in the balloon over his head. It was just a cartoon I did, and then the painting was based on it: the same fat-faced politician standing up at a banquet table and making a speech to his cronies, all of them in formal dress, with a yellow curtain behind them. I suppose it is an indictment of these people, but it was influenced by the gangster movies being made by Hollywood around that time.

I've always loved these character actors that used to play the wonderful bit parts in these films. And in this sense, it is not a bitter indictment. There's comedy too. I wouldn't call it black comedy, either. There's a familiarity about them. You couldn't grow up in Boston without having a kind of scornful affection for these characters.

opposite:

THE CARD PLAYERS ca. 1940
Gouache on paper, 16¾ x 21¼ in.
Whereabouts unknown

THE CARD PLAYERS 1941
Oil on canvas, 15⅜ x 13¼ in.
Whereabouts unknown

DRAMATIS PERSONAE ca. 1942
Oil on board, 5½ x 11½ in.
University of Arizona Museum of Art, Tucson
Gift of C. Leonard Pfeiffer

35

THE PASSING SCENE 1941
Oil on composition board, 48 x 39¾ in.
The Museum of Modern Art, New York

I was going into the army, and I painted an old man and a young boy. It was a bit like the three ages of man, but with myself *subtracted* from it. So what I had here was a kind of a small tenement like they have in Boston, and a clothesline in back and the old horse, which I always saw as a beautiful, tender symbol—a white horse. And there were pieces of lath, and there's a garbage can with a crumpled newspaper hanging out of it and showing a headline about Tula, which was at that time the furthest point the Panzer divisions had reached on the Eastern front. As I say, I'm there by inference, having been subtracted.

KING JOSIAH 1941
Oil on paper, 13½ x 11¾ in.
Sid Deutsch Gallery, New York

THE KING 1945
Oil on panel, 10 x 7 in.
Whereabouts unknown

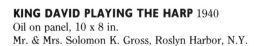

KING DAVID PLAYING THE HARP 1940
Oil on panel, 10 x 8 in.
Mr. & Mrs. Solomon K. Gross, Roslyn Harbor, N.Y.

My father's death in 1939 started me on the path of painting these Jewish sages. It was his religion, not mine, but when he died I felt like I was scoring points for him, because I had a good relationship with him, and with my mother too. Should I do a *Deborah* someday because of my mother? I probably owe it.

During this period, I always kept these paintings of kings and other biblical scenes small. I was doing much of this biblical stuff because I was very much involved with the way the Flemish painted, and the way the Persians did—

the Mughal paintings and such. I was trying to do something like that. It was much easier if you wanted to be influenced by Van Eyck or Van der Weyden to paint men with beards and turbans. If you're interested in Mughal painting, Rajput painting, you were dealing with something similar. It wasn't Judaism bursting out of me, but a kind of museumology. I suppose that there's one of these little paintings after another where I was able to record something I had seen in museums and to some degree to make it my own. So, in a sense, it's a confrontation. I remember being very impressed with what the art historian Erwin Panofsky said one time: "I'm an artist without hands." And I thought, "By God, I'm an historian with hands." In a way, my involvement with the Jews is political, and in a way history-mongering. It brings me closer to some kind of artistic precedent I have my eye on. But as for people who say I shouldn't be involved with gold-leaf backgrounds and Hebrew letters, and then with beards and turbans making hieratic gestures, the hell with those people.

HORSE 1947 ▶
Charcoal on paper, 23 x 30 in.
Whereabouts unknown

Commentary on

THE PENSIONNAIRE
THE WHITE HORSE

The first painting I did when I got out of the army was *The Pensionnaire*, an old man in front of an old two-story house, with a church steeple in the background. It has a certain kinship with some of my early Judaica paintings, and it also shows my continuing involvement with some kind of Romantic traditionalism. I painted it in the Renaissance way, beginning with monochrome and carrying it into color. *The White Horse* was a reprise of the background from *The Passing Scene*, which I'd done four years before. You see, I hadn't really painted in three and a half years, and it was a matter of sounding certain notes again.

PLANNING KING SOLOMON'S TEMPLE 1941
Oil on masonite, 10 x 8 in.
The Israel Museum, Jerusalem

THE PENSIONNAIRE 1945
Oil on masonite, 36 x 28 in.
Sheldon Memorial Art Gallery
University of Nebraska-Lincoln
F. M. Hall Collection

HORSE AND WAGON ca. 1947
Oil on canvas
Whereabouts and size unknown

THE WHITE HORSE 1946
Oil on canvas, 30 x 36 in.
University of Oklahoma Museum
of Art, Norman, Oklahoma

GENTLEMAN FROM THE SOUTH 1946
Oil on masionite, 22 x 15 in.
Dr. & Mrs. J. B. Yasinow, Philadelphia

AID TO DIGESTION 1946
Oil on paper, 31 x 22 in.
Private collection

Gentleman from the South is an imaginary portrait of a prototypical Southerner, from the viewpoint of an outsider—of a Northeasterner from Boston, living in New York, who doesn't identify with the people from other regions of America. At that time, I knew Zero Mostel (who was a painter as well as an actor) and had seen some comedy skits in which he played a Southerner, and I had heard the wonderful Senator Claghorn character on Fred Allen's radio show. I remember a routine where one of these characters was asked about conditions in the South and he replied, "Suh, down South we have no conditions." I had seen the South when I was a soldier, having been stationed in five southern states, and I was appalled by the conditions imposed by segregation. Which is not to say that the situation up North was all that great either. I've been to the South several times since then, and, frankly, I think it's much improved.

THE BANQUET 1939
Pencil on paper, 10 x 14⅟₁₆ in.
Addison Gallery of American Art
Phillips Academy, Andover Massachusetts

WELCOME HOME 1946
Oil on canvas, 40 x 60 in.
The Brooklyn Museum

My whole social outlook had vaporized during three and a half years in the army, during which I didn't see a child, I didn't see a black. I was essentially in confinement, very much as though I were on a prison island. In fact I was on a desert island for 20 months. When I came out of the army I had two feelings considering the sort of career I had. One was enormous elation at being out. And the other was this kind of tight-lipped thing about the whole caste system in the army. I hated officers.

So I painted this picture called *Welcome Home*. We were all coming back, and tugboats were blowing whistles and there were streamers saying welcome home Luigi, welcome home Abe, welcome home whoever; and I thought, as a satirist, that it was just for me to welcome home a returning general. I remember that I had done a drawing many years ago of people sitting at dinner, chew-

ing, very much like cattle at a fence. And incidentally, in *Welcome Home* I painted the first woman I ever included in a multi-figure composition. And I was greeting a major-general who had just returned.

Some officers lived in a world of their own creation. This general has come home and he's still in that sort of a world. I'm not talking about men like Bradley and Eisenhower. I have great respect for them. It's just the big slob who is vice-president of the Second National Bank and president of the Chamber of Commerce, only now he's been in the army. I couldn't say that sort of thing while I was in the service. This was my time to howl.

Welcome Home later became an international controversy when the State Department of the United States sent an exhibition of American art to Moscow in 1959. The House Un-American Affairs Committee charged that many of the American artists whose works were in the show had pro-Communist affiliations, and it was going to conduct an investigation. There was a big commotion about it in the press. Evergood and Shahn and I were

subpoenaed to appear before the committee (but I was in Spain with my family at the time, and nothing ever came of it). I wouldn't have chosen to send *Welcome Home* there in the first place. If they'd asked me, I would have chosen something a bit more diplomatic. So here we were, as somebody pointed out, corrupting all these Russians toward Communism. And in the meantime, President Eisenhower had a press conference. May Craig, a Maine newspaper woman, pointed out that my painting lampoons an American general and she asked him what he thought of that. "Well," Eisenhower said, "it is not a painting in the classical sense of the word. It is a sort of lampoon." And then the curator of American art in Moscow fired back, "A lot of people don't like *his* paintings either." (You know, Eisenhower was painting pictures by numbers.) And the Russians who came to the exhibition kept counting the paintings, to see if mine had been removed. Same number of paintings. And the American curator that sassed the President was still sitting there at the desk. So I think if there was a salubrious lesson here, it was for the Russians.

THE RELUCTANT PLOUGHSHARE 1946
Gouache, 19 x 22 in.
IBM Corporation Armonk, N.Y.

I did a gouache after *Welcome Home*, a pendant to it, so to speak, and I called it *The Reluctant Ploughshare*. I think it's one of my best titles. It's like what Jack Benny once said—if he can't take it with him, he don't go. The point here is that he is not going to give up the sword. He doesn't want to beat it into a ploughshare, he doesn't want to be a farmer. The pay's too good in the army.

It sometimes happened that after I finished a painting, I found the theme particularly rich, and I'd do studies *after* it, as I did here, taking certain ideas and elements and developing them a bit differently. However, although I sometimes did a number of drawings and sketches as studies for a large painting—and sometimes I'd even do a painting of some of the figures before trying the whole composition—I never based it on a single elaborately planned study, because I don't like the idea of executing a big canvas from a small maquette. I remember this painter who described somebody as having left his fight in the gym, and he worked so hard that when he got into the ring he had nothing left. I prefer to solve my problems directly on the canvas.

MARS CONFOUNDED 1946
Oil on canvas, 18 x 22 in.
Whereabouts unknown

Study for MARS CONFOUNDED 1946
Oil on canvas, 18 x 22 in.
Whereabouts unknown

Commentary on
MARS CONFOUNDED
WARRIOR'S RETURN

Mars Confounded and *Warrior's Return* are both in that classical, allegorical vein that I've assayed from time to time. They both have to do with love and war, and you can see in them a new sensuality, which comes from my having begun to paint the female body. I had never painted a woman in any of my group compositions until *Welcome Home*. I may have done a drawing of a woman or something like that, but that was the first in a large formal canvas. And then it happens more often. *Mars Confounded* was the first time I'd integrated a nude into a composition. I had been painting guys in derby hats— you know, thugs, politicans, unshaven goons, whatever. How was I going to work nice nudes into my paintings? Obviously, I had to take that long step. So I started doing these classical allegories, such as *Mars Confounded* and *Homage to Boston*.

WARRIOR'S RETURN (Battle's End) 1946–48
Oil on canvas, 20 x 24 in.
Collection of the artist

Then, there is the problem of painting from life, anyway. There is a problem of how the nude fits, and there is also the problem of being able to do a design at all if you are dependent on the figure in front of you. Rembrandt always painted from models, I think, but then he could do a sketch—a very relaxed sketch of, perhaps, a dozen people—in about a minute and a half. So, obviously, he could also draw without a model. It became a matter of professional pride with me that I do not need a model either.

I actually did *Warrior's Return* to commemorate my getting out of the army and getting married. The golden angel is supposed to be Ruth, and the brute in armor is supposed to be me. The two figures don't look like either of us, but it didn't matter. It was done with my sense of new freedom in mind, and my sense of new marriage. Although I had mixed feelings about being married, I was happy with Ruth. But even then, I had no idea how much she was going to mean to me as time went by.

Commentary on
MAGIC FOR THE MILLIONS

My first trip to Europe strengthened my resolution to learn all I could about the great art of the past, and to try to get closer to the artists whom I admired. *Magic for the Millions* is a pastiche of El Greco, with an emphasis on elongated forms, a motif of ascending flames, and his particular way of working—that is, using a reddish base tone, warm light colors on top of cold grays, and a dead wine-color transparency over that, with shots of blue interspersed here and there. You can also see the Expressionist influence here, in the crawling brushstrokes and the release of my own energy, which has a certain equivalent in the loose brushwork and unrestrained virtuosity of El Greco, Tintoretto, and other Baroque masters. At the same time, you can also see my hunger for a kind of measured classicism, a desire to balance this exuberant style with a sense of rational stability. In fact, Tintoretto had that balance, but in general the Baroque period was characterized by showmanship, with most artists abandoning sobriety and the simple virtues for inflated rhetoric and flashier entertainment values. In a way, they were like Madison Avenue hucksters, who try to sell people what they don't need; all that talent and technique was put to the service of getting people into the churches, stirring up their emotions, and sweeping them away with glamorized images of religious doctrine. The medium was the message. Rational thought was considered inimical to faith. In terms of theme, I was expressing my complete rejection of religious myticism by showing the human race being flimflammed by their own beliefs. So, instead of one of El Greco's ecstatic visions, I have a magician pulling a rabbit out of a hat, and a crowd of people around him who are convinced that they are seeing something supernatural. I pride myself on being a rationalist (I don't dread black cats walking in front of me, and I sometimes do walk under ladders), and here I deliberately chose to debunk the idea of the religious miracle and the notion of "divine manifestation."

TOMBSTONE CUTTER 1947
Oil on canvas, 36 x 30 in.
Midtown Galleries, New York

When I painted *Tombstone Cutter*, I think I'd seen some pictures of the graveyard in Prague, and perhaps I was thinking of my father, who had died several years earlier. And there used to be tombstone cutters on Houston street near where Ruth and I used to live on the Lower East Side. And it all came together. I thought I would make an analogy between the gnarled old body and these Prague tombstones. On the formal level, I was trying to show some kind of stability in disorder, to express the possibility of a theme and a countertheme in the same painting. No matter how gnarled and knotted it is, the basic format of horizontals and verticals is very measured. Now, looking at it, however, I think it's still a bit disorderly, if the truth be told.

MAGIC FOR THE MILLIONS 1948
Oil on canvas, 49½ x 19⅜ in.
Seattle Art Muesum
Gift of Mrs. Sidney Gerber and the late Mr. Gerber

APTEKA 1947
Oil on canvas, 40 x 60 in.
Whereabouts unknown

I always tended to paint about corrupt politics. I'm from Boston so I know about such things. In Boston you always hear cynicism about what's going on in the State House, or in City Hall. You will hear it on all sides. The radical thing I did was to put it on canvas and present it as a work of fine art, which was considered bad form. You're not supposed to paint about it. You can grumble, and you can write a letter to the papers, but you're not suppose to paint a big picture about it—that's considered dirty pool.

I did a painting of a Polish drugstore called *Apteka*. I liked the word "apteka." It is like "apothecary." It's sort of tripping on the tongue. It was a charming green storefront, with a kind of fluting, a wonderful kind of classical architecture. It was in the South End of Boston and I was mindful of the fact that in the South End they have brick sidewalks. You don't see that too much in New York. So I have this pink sidewalk, and I have red danger flags because they're digging up the streets, so there were barriers, sawhorses, and red flags, and *Time* Magazine denounced *Apteka* as a soap box painting. They said the painting was seething in anger, or something like that and they referred to me as "angry Jack Levine." There was a certain amount of red in it. There was this very intense pink sidewalk, and there were red flags, and so forth, and there was a fire box. There were also some oranges, and some greens, and some golds. But there was all this red against it. They didn't say anything about the greens, only the reds.

WOODSTOCK PASTORALE 1949
Oil on canvas, 25 x 31 in.
The Fine Arts Museum of San Francisco
Mildred Anna Williams Collection

In *Woodstock Pastorale* I was trying to get some of the same qualities that I've seen in Rubens. I chose a subject that might be conducive to paint that way, just as I've said about these Jewish kings I did. I've always been very much involved with Old Master techniques, and have never been in the slightest interested in contemporary techniques, because I don't think anybody can do anything much nowadays. But back in the 1920s, a man named Jacques Maroger started doing research into Old Master techniques and became quite an expert (he later became technical director of the Louvre's laboratory, and president of the Restorers of France, and he published a book call *The Secret Formulas and Techniques of the Masters).* A lot of artists were using the medium that he recommended, known as black oil. Principally it consists of oil that has been mixed with lead—Litharge (which is red lead) or white lead—and then cooked until it is the color of black coffee. Augustus John used it, Raoul Dufy used it. And a lot of artists here, such as Reginald Marsh and John Koch, tried it, and I tried my hand at it too.

HOMAGE TO BOSTON 1949
Oil on canvas, 20 x 50⅛ in.
Hirshhorn Museum and Sculpture Garden,
Smithsonian Institution
Gift of Joseph H. Hirshhorn, 1966

Back in 1949 I still considered myself a Bostonian. That was before it became a combat zone. It was still prim in those days. I was teaching at the American Art School for a while and would go there two mornings a week. There, mind you, my students were working from lovely models, while I had no such luxury in my life here in New York. Feeling a bit jealous, I began to draw some lines on a canvas to show how I would pose the model I intended to hire from the life-class. Before I knew it, the painting was underway without a model. While I was working, the thought of "Venice, Queen of the Adriatic" came to mind and it occurred to me that it would be a nice bit of satire for me to pay tribute to "Boston, Queen of the Fish Industry" or something like that. I filled up the background with buildings, like the Old State House, the Commonwealth Pier, the Park Street Meeting House, specifics I had to do research on. Yes, I don't mind saying that if I am going to paint a picture of Faneuil Hall, I need a picture of it, but if it's a woman holding Faneuil Hall in the palm of her hand, I don't need a picture of her. That I would rather do myself.

EVERY INCH A RULER (The End of the Line) 1948
Oil on canvas, 36 x 24 in.
The Phillips Collection, Washington, D.C.

Study for RECEPTION IN MIAMI 1947
Brown ink on gray paper, 15⅝ x 22⅝ in.
Fogg Art Museum, Harvard University, Cambridge, MA
Gift of Meta and Paul J. Sachs

RECEPTION IN MIAMI 1948
Gouache on cardboard, 15 x 21⅞ in.
Sheldon Memorial Art Gallery, University of Nebraska-Lincoln
F.M. Hall Collection

I remember thinking at one point as I was working on this painting that I must have been pretty hard up for ideas to go against the divine right of kings. Although the painting itself is actually pretty good, it really wasn't much of a topic—how royalty is degenerate and played out, plagued by hemophilia as a result of inbreeding, and so forth. The alternate title, *The End of the Line*, indicated my rejoicing in the final demise of the ancestral aristocracy, but I don't care for it much. The original title, *Every Inch a Ruler*, may be a bad joke (which someone evidently thought it was, perhaps rightfully so, and thus asked me to change it), but sometimes you can be too *raffiné*. The Phillips Gallery is delighted with the original title, so perhaps its time has come.

Reception in Miami was the result of reading one day in Earl Wilson's column in the *New York Post* that the Duke and Duchess of Windsor had come to Miami, and that at one of their appearances in the lobby there was much bowing and curtsying on the part of our fellow Americans. I thought this disgusting. That was the basis for something like a drawing-room comedy, with all kinds of effete snobs (as someone said later) bowing and scraping, like puppets at the end of a string, and becoming British subjects for the evening. I thought that was a good topic. I think I probably considered my entry into any painting on the basis of subject matter. It's something I would never discard. Subject matter is all important.

RECEPTION IN MIAMI 1948
Oil on canvas, 50⅜ x 56⅛ in.
Hirshhorn Museum and Sculpture Garden, Smithsonian Institution
Gift of Joseph H. Hirshhorn, 1966

The '50s

By the 1950s I had been to Europe, and I had seen the great Italian frescoes and the great Dutch paintings, and I had a sense of having encountered the reality of history, more than I could get in the Boston Museum or the Metropolitan Museum of Art. When I received a Fulbright grant in 1951, Ruth and I went back to Europe and lived in Rome for a year, and when we returned to New York I began to realize that the Abstract Expressionist movement had frozen, I wouldn't say *under* me, but *over* me. I began to realize that I was out in the cold; it was a very depressing feeling. The Eighth Street Club, the Cedar Tavern boys, had really taken over, and I was an outsider from then on, as far as what was considered valid as art—that is, what was considered the rage, the thing to do. It was never going to be me again, I could see that. In fact, no one was ever going to train that much.

As far as joining with other artists on an aesthetic basis, with one exception, I had contempt for that. I had contempt for the movement, for the movement stars, for bandwagons, for fashion. But I did get involved with other artists, on a political basis or on a basis of the economic needs of the artist. I got involved with a publication called *Reality*, which Raphael Soyer was a part of, that tried to get some kind of consideration for something other than Abstract Expressionism, which became absolutely dominant in the '50s. I even went in a delegation to the Museum of Modern Art for some other artists; as it turned out, my participation was considered important because I was the only one in the delegation who was represented in the Museum.

From a political aspect, since I'm supposed to be a political thinker, from time to time I managed to strike a political note in my work. It's important to point out that for me there was always an element of expedience about my subject matter. I mean, I was interested in the political scene as a subject very much because I felt it might give rise to a dramatic tableau, just as a lot of my co-ethnics, Jewish people that is, thought that I did this Judaica because I'm a good Jew and might be pious, when the fact of the matter is that it gave me access to material that I had a legitimate right to. I remember one young man who made a nine-day sensation and he liked to lard his paintings with letters in Greek, and since he was not a Greek there was something spurious about it. I always contended that all this business with bearded men in turbans and with Hebrew lettering was legitimately mine. But you see it enabled me to deal with subject matter and to study and utilize techniques of Northern European painting of the 15th and 16th centuries and Persian miniatures. It was an enabling thing, in much the same way my political interests enabled me to arrive at something like *Gangster Funeral, Inauguration,* and *Election Night.* I don't know why it was possible to make films in the '30s, gangster films and such, which were rich in character and some kinds of sour humor, without Hollywood particularly taking a strong political line. But for some reason or other I had to see it as a political line—that and as a projection of *The Threepenny Opera.* What was important was to expose social injustice. I've always tried to be forthright and legitimate in all matters, but I tend to accentuate the negative. One fears to be a Norman Rockwell. However, I think we'll find that Norman Rockwell was a critic too. It's going to amount to a vast, many-sided statement about platitudes in America, if *only* that. For my part I think it's safer to be negative, especially in the 20th century. There's plenty to be negative about, except that in the long run it's the same thing. It depends on your personality. To be positive about an evil, to be accepting about an evil, is the *ultimate* cynicism. That's obvious enough. I mean, I'm not a cynic, because I won't accept rottenness.

After the war, a tremendous number of people who'd been in the army came back and started families, and they all wanted to have their children grow up in the country, which I'm convinced is the worst place for children to grow up. (Now those same people are moving back to town so they can walk to work and live like human beings and not spend their lives behind a wheel. A dear friend of mine, now dead, had to drive three hours every day or be in a train just to get where his children could grow up under trees.) The adversity of the Depression and wartime had kept them from living the lives they wanted. It was just a certain striving for the good life, and everybody wanted the same thing. I think that compared to now it wasn't a period of comformity. The '80s is a period of conformity. Of course you had the witch-hunting, and you had McCarthyism and all that, and people had been shut up. Those were trying times. But I wouldn't call that conformity so much as intimidation. There was a lot of that. And you'd think twice before you said something. I think that I tended to paint whatever I wanted to, but I think painting is a little bit more inscrutable.

THE ABUNDANT LIFE 1950
Oil on canvas, 30 x 36 in.
Mr. & Mrs. Joseph Strick

I had heard a remark by President Truman implying that anybody who talked about poverty during his administration must be un-American, so I immediately decided to paint a pawnshop. Part of my impulse in doing that was political, but I was also showing off a bit with some of the knowledge I'd acquired when I was in Italy. *Abundant Life* features a plaster cast of Lorenzo de Medici in a window, and the three balls of the pawnshop, which is the Medici coat of arms. I was being a little bit learned there. But that painting led to my doing the big *Pawnshop,* which I finished in Rome a year later.

PAWNSHOP 1951
Oil on canvas, 80 x 96 in.
Whereabouts unknown

Commentary on **PAWNSHOP**
UNDER THE EL

Pawnshop was my brief honeymoon with Cubism. It was an experiment in using a fractured surface, with all sorts of shattered and overlapping planes, but with the white of the primed canvas showing through around every object, as, for example, Braque might have done. Although I had started *Pawnshop* in New York, I did most of it the year I was in Rome, and I finished it there. I chose the subject deliberately for its critical social implications; you can't get away from the idea of poverty in a pawnshop. Perhaps I

hadn't realized that I was also depicting a collection of objects that allude to certain aspects of civilization, of human history—clarinets and guitars and cameras and fishing rods and saxophones and accordions, whatever people pawned—but I suppose that that kind of Cubist idiom is a way of listing all of these things with equanimity. It creates a certain detachment. However, although in certain cases (like some of Picasso's portraits) Cubism gives a rather strong reading on the painting's subject, for the most part I think it tends to obfuscate. As far as I'm concerned, it's a dead end as a style; all it did was obscure the point I was trying to make. The cubes and planes and

UNDER THE EL, 1952
Oil on canvas, 36 x 58 in.
The Phillips Collection, Washington, D.C.

alarm clocks created by man to conquer the problems of this life are for me secondary objects of contemplation. And the idea of pure painting—by that I mean painting unallied with anything else, abstraction—is anathema to me.

Pawnshop didn't signal a turn toward abstraction; in fact, I moved away from the approach I was trying there. When I came back to New York, I went back to another painting in a similar vein, also of a pawnshop, with the same kinds of fractured forms, and that became a painting called *Under the El.* It began with high colors—a bright blue sky, cobalt, cadmiums for flesh—and as I worked on it, it took on a Rembrandt atmosphere, as if it might be under the El, and a fractured surface with all sorts of shattered and overlapping planes. These changes constituted, more than anything else, a revaluation of light and shadow for its exciting potentialities in making a picture. This use of light and shadow has two functions: it thrusts the im-

age into structural saliency, and it produces a dynamic arabesque across the surface. The projection of shadows gives you the image along with the other aspects, for you can disintegrate an image and still have the image. Within light and shadow I can express some kind of drama which is most like me. *Pawnshop* was very *concrète*; but at the same time, I hadn't given up on the idea of expressionism. In *Under the El* I was moving toward a third approach, a kind of dramatic realism, which is neither really one or the other, possibly partaking of both. The next painting after *Under the El* was *Gangster Funeral*, where I tried to get far away from any kind of 20th-century mannerisms which I felt obscured content. Sometimes I've experimented with an approach in order to discover its possibilities, or its lack of possibilities—to confirm to myself why I should *not* do it. It may be a direction or a rebound from a direction. But ultimately, my intention is to bring the great tradition, with whatever is great about it, up to date.

THE GOLDEN ANATOMY LESSON, 1952
Oil on canvas, 42 x 48 in.
Munson-Williams-Proctor Institute Museum of Art
Utica, New York

Living in Rome, I was very conscious of what I thought was American imperialism. I had some dim idea that the American ruling class was conquering the world and dividing it up. My version of Rembrandt's *The Golden Helmet* is a kind of Midas-like American imperialism. Well, I don't think we divided the world very much, but that was my view at the time. *The Golden Anatomy Lesson* is another reprise of *The Feast of Pure Reason*, except this time there are four figures instead of three. One of them is Truman, whom I always thought of as a second-rate character. I may have been wrong, but I didn't look at him with much admiration. I put a golden helmet on him,

which to me was like something out of Upton Sinclair. Perhaps it's a kind of tired symbolism, but I'm guilty of it. And then there's a banker, and on the left, in a white naval uniform, is James Forrestal. The fourth figure is Henry Wallace. I don't know what Henry Wallace is doing there.

He's supposed to be a liberal, and I remember doing something for Wallace's candidacy, but I guess I decided that things were more complicated than I had believed. I now think that things are even more complicated than I thought *then*. For the background I chose the coffered

ceiling of the Pantheon, which after all is Roman empire. So my symbols of empire consist of a mighty coffered dome, and the golden helmet, and the globe, which is all cut and splintered in a kind of Cubist business, like slicing a sphere, to give a squared-off solidity to the facets.

THE HUMANIST 1951
Oil on canvas, 35 x 27½ in.
Whereabouts unknown

The subject of the humanist is one that I have been attracted to frequently: the ancient scribe, the prophet writing, the contemplative wise man. It's a more freely painted version of what I've attempted before and since in the miniatures that I've done—like one of those gone wild. This turbaned figure wearing a quilted jerkin is at a desk (the same sort of desk I depicted in *Hillel* and *Maimonides*), writing with a quill pen, and behind him is an astrolabe—an instrument used to determine the position of heavenly bodies—and a telescope. Before and after *The Humanist* I was working on *Pawnshop*, which, in its Cubist splintering of image and surface, was an essay in modernism but which was also classical—School of Paris, 20th-century classical—with a firm, geometric stability. In *The Humanist* I was employing a different approach, painting certain images on top of other half-painted images, and using a somewhat frenetic brushstroke and colors that screamed a bit—for example, flaming vermilion against a loud pink. Although the style is rather free, at the time I painted it I wasn't yet so aware of what the Abstract Expressionists were doing, but it wasn't too long before I realized that I could never follow their example, because they relinquished too much of the subject.

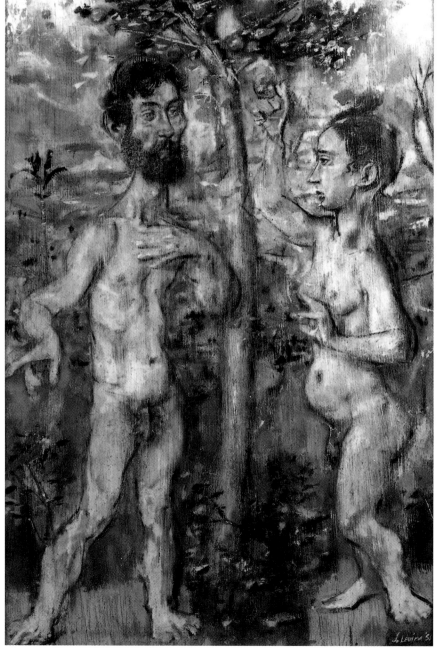

ADAM AND EVE 1951
Oil on wood, 10 x 8 in.
Dr. Steven Palumbo, New York

When I was younger, I had it instilled in me that my paintings might have a socially didactic purpose, and as time went on I began to realize that themes from the Old Testament might have more to do with the nature of man and with human desires than anything projected by the social upheavals of my time. I found that there are certain needs, many of which I myself felt, that were not answered by any of the movements that were going on. The kind of material offered by the theme of Adam and Eve, for example, represented a rest from the social sermons I'd undertaken so often. In a sense, it was a form of recreation; I did it to please myself. Perhaps I'd seen a wonderful Cranach or van der Goes that set me off, although I didn't have any particular model in mind while I was doing it; it was an improvisation. And by keeping the scale modest, I could hold it in one hand while I painted with the other, which makes an enormous difference. I was also trying to teach myself a procedure of painting akin to the way the early Flemish or Dutch masters worked, so that it would develop organicaly and have something of the quality of the paintings I'd seen in museums. Here, as I recall, I did a highly detailed drawing in dark brown oil on a white gesso ground, and over that I laid a thin tone across the entire surface, and then I began to paint. I think I painted the figures first, although a real professional would probably do the background first. The final result wasn't bad, but I really believe I know more now than I did then.

MAIMONIDES 1952
Oil on panel, 10 x 8 in.
The Jewish Theological Seminary
of America, New York

Commentary on
MAIMONIDES
KING SAUL
KING ASA

In *Maimonides, King Saul,* and *King Asa,* I returned to biblical figures not for any particular reason in the subject but simply because they set me off. These subjects, these formats, these sizes are all enabling things. I certainly haven't gone into Judaica out of some sort of religious piety. There are craft reasons—textures to deal with and atmospheric passages to paint, and even the way the paint is dealt with. The sense of scale is involved too, for these are in a sense miniatures. If I were commissioned to do a contemporary portrait in the same manner, I wouldn't have accepted. As I have often explained, I would not be able to do this if I had painted John D. Rockefeller in a tweed suit. That would not enable me to handle the technical material that was involved.

Maimonides was a 12th-century Spanish-born scholar and physician, author of a philosophical treatise, *Guide to the Perplexed* (in which he can be seen as a forerunner of Spinoza), and one of the luminaries of the great Arab renaissance that took place while most of Europe was in the throes of what we commonly refer to as the Dark Ages. I painted a hill with houses in the background of *Maimonides,* way off in the distance, and when I finally saw the Mount of Olives in Jerusalem on my fifth trip to Israel, I was reminded of my own painting.

King Saul is rather ferocious, and that is what I tried to convey. The helmet, the bow and quiver, and the rest of his costume suggest Persia. The colors of this costume are quite vivid, and the dark gray-blue background serves as an effective foil. The sharply defined diagonal behind him is in the tradition of the Oriental system of perspective which uses an upward movement to convey the notion of moving backward into the pictorial space.

Asa was that rare thing, a good king. Here I have shown him as a benign old man in a scene of contemplation. His name appears in Hebrew at the upper left. I also painted the Hebrew phrase for "watchtower" to his left, just above the domed tower or cupola in the landscape behind him, and another that says "the Heights of Benjamin" to his right, just above a configuration of green cypress and poplar trees that resembles a Chinese ideogram.

To me, these figures with beards and turbans were part of the endless flow of history. They went way back to antiquity and at the same time they were as familiar as the elderly Jews that I used to see at the synagogue my father took me to when I was a child. The date of the setting of these paintings is really of no great consequence; it might just as well be Flanders in the 16th century as Israel in ancient time, or even in the present.

Each one deals with a fresh problem. *King Saul* is the one with the flattest background, the one most sectioned off into flat planes. *King Asa* shows a flat miniature style with rounded forms, like a medallion. *Maimonides* is the one in which I dealt most with form shading into shadow. With each painting, my performance became more knowledgeable in terms of reconstruction of the old traditional methods. *Maimonides* was actually the last of the three, and by then I had given up the use of gold leaf, just as the van Eycks had at a certain point in their development, although I'd enjoyed it in the paintings where I did use it. It's just oil gilding—gold leaf slapped onto sticky oil paint—but it was a lot of fun and it added a certain element of splendor. It was another color value to work with, a kind of warm reflection, in addition to the primary and secondary colors and black and white. These three paintings show a greater technical proficiency and refinement since I had painted *Shelomo* and *King David* a dozen years earlier. All of them are studies in flat-pattern painting with nuanced drawing, and all of them are part of my education in Old Master techniques and my constant attempt to explain to myself some of the mysteries of 15th- and 16th-century Flemish art. The art of the van Eycks is at least as difficult to understand as the making of a Stradivarius.

KING SAUL 1952
Oil on panel, 13¾ x 11 in.
Midtown Galleries, New York

KING ASA 1953
Oil on canvas board, 10 x 8 in.
The Harvard University Art Museums (Fogg Art Museum)
Bequest of Meta and Paul J. Sachs

THE OFFERING 1953
Oil on canvas, 39 x 24 in.
Private collection

THE MOURNER 1952
Charcoal and pastel on paper, 23 x 18 in.
Whereabouts unknown

above right:

Study for GANGSTER FUNERAL
Charcoal on paper, 19 x 24¾ in.
The Montclair Art Museum, New Jersey
Bequest of Ida and Moses Soyer

THE MAN WITH THE STAINED GLASS EYE 1952
Oil on canvas, 25 x 19 in.
Hirshhorn Museum and Sculpture Garden, Smithsonian Institution
Gift of Joseph H. Hirshhorn, 1966

THE MOURNER (Study for GANGSTER FUNERAL) 1954–55
Oil on canvas, 39 x 22 in.
Private collection

I did a painting of a gangster funeral around 1952. Chronologically, in American art, it comes after the movies *Public Enemy* (1931) and *A Slight Case of Murder* (1938) but before *The Last Hurrah* (1958) and *Some Like It Hot* (1959). A lot of my characters were drawn from the old gangster movies of the 1930s. There is a little guy with a dyed mustache and false teeth, who combed his hair across his skull. I have always loved him. There is a man in the painting who looks like Brian Donleavy in *The Great McGinty* and who also looks like our former mayor of New York, big Bill O'Dwyer, who ran off to Mexico City with our subway money. Then there is a kind of dualism.

There is a man shown up close that looks like a Boston politician—maybe Dowd or Beano Breen—and he is drawn toward the corpse while at the same time he is pulling away in fear. I rather like that. A policeman of high rank stands in the background among the mourners, and another man—sort of a red-haired, turnip-headed guy—is next to the body, keeping an eye on the proceedings, so to speak. The corpse is shown head first, because I am not interested in depicting anything macabre, anything that would frighten the children. I want to state it but not show it, to get behind it as soon as possible. I want the painting as a comedy. It must not be a tragedy. I will show the

corpse, but the emphasis could be on the embalming. The coloration overall is that found in an undertaker's reposing room. As one critic said, "Levine is not interested in 'color color.'" That's true; I am interested in funeral-home color, like the handsome, quiet colors used for the decor of reposing rooms. *Gangster Funeral* is a picture which I did because it is typical of America and I am glad I made the comment.

At the time I was painting it, I wrote the following remarks, which I delivered at a symposium at the Museum of Modern Art: "I should like to paint a narrative because it is possible for adolescents to buy marihuana and cocaine

59

GANGSTER FUNERAL 1952–53
Oil on canvas, 63 x 72 in.
Whitney Museum of American Art

GANGSTER FUNERAL (detail)

on our streets with the connivance and the complacency of the powers-that-be. Consequently, I am at work on a painting of a 'Gangster Funeral.' Immediately such questions arise such as what sort of dress shall be worn. What do people wear at a gangster funeral? This may seem a concern for a dramatist, a novelist. I envy them these interesting concerns. If they be wearing street clothes instead of cutaways, it becomes possible to have the fat man show a broad mourning band on his thick little arm. It would be amusing to make it a heart instead of a band, but unfortunately, that isn't possible. A widow. In deep mourning, clad in rich furs. Better yet, two widows. One very, very shapely. The chief of police, come to pay his last respects—a face at once porcine and acute—under no circumstances off to one side as a watcher. This would suggest a thesis other than mine, a policeman's thesis. He must be in the line of mourners, filing past to view for the last time the earthly remains of his old associate, who would, if he could, remonstrate with him for exposing himself in such a manner. If the chief's function is thus made clear then it becomes possible to add a pair of men in a watchful capacity. I must now look for ways of establishing the identities of the mayor, the governor, et alia. It may be said that the idea is more fit for a novel or a film. This is ridiculous. As far as a novel is concerned, a picture is still worth a thousand words; as far as a film is concerned, the Hays Code requires it to show that crime does not pay, which is not my thesis either. The libretto in no way invalidates the possible creation of a work of art. On the contrary, it inflects it, it enriches it, it makes the project more complex. I see no harm in putting the conscious mind to work in this fashion."

First draft for GANGSTER FUNERAL 1952
Gouache on paper, 20½ x 25 in.
Whereabouts unknown

COURTROOM STUDY 1953
Oil on canvas, 36 x 40 in.
Mr. & Mrs. Peter Blum

opposite above:

Study for GANGSTER FUNERAL 1953
Oil on canvas, 35 x 40 in.
University of Iowa Museum of Art, Iowa City

opposite below right:

GANGSTER WEDDING 1957
Oil on canvas, 16 x 14 in.
Midtown Galleries, New York

Commentary on
COURTHOUSE STUDY
THE JUDGE
THE TRIAL

After I did *Gangster Funeral* and the other paintings related to that theme, I began to think about doing a courtroom painting, and the result was *The Trial* and a couple of other paintings around that time. I didn't even know what the inside of a courtroom looked like, as I'd never been in one. (I hadn't yet been called for jury duty at that time.) I'd always been leery about places like police

stations and courtrooms, so instead of going downtown and visiting one of the courthouses there, I was trying to get lawyers I knew to describe the way a typical courtroom is laid out—the jury box, the lawyers' tables, where the witness sits in relation to the judge, and so forth. In 1953 I was teaching at Skowhegan, and a socially prominent woman came to my studio with Judge Learned Hand (who was probably the most distinguished American legal mind since Brandeis and Cardozo). I happened to be working on one of these courtroom paintings, and when he saw it he became very angry because I had included an armed policeman in the scene, and he told me that he would

THE JUDGE 1953
Oil on canvas, 42 x 48 in.
Williams College Museum of Art
Bequest of Lawrence H. Bloedel, '23

never allow that in his court. He was horrified at the idea of armed force in the courtroom. I was very embarrassed at my own ignorance. I didn't really know anything about the procedures, the architecture, or the choreography of a courtroom. I just went ahead with what I had, informing myself as I went. Although the anti-Communist "witch hunts" of Sen. Joseph McCarthy had something to do with *The Trial*, the emotional charge was basically the horror of the execution of the Rosenbergs. I think if it hadn't been for that I wouldn't have felt pressed to do it. Now I've said that I seem to be unable to paint a subject picture without somehow backing into the iconography of Christian art. *Gangster Funeral*, for instance, is a deposition. In *The Trial*, the way I conceived of it, the judge is another Christian symbol. Here, I've modeled him after the judge who presided over the 1947 Red trials, Harold Medina, who I think is in a way reminiscent of Groucho Marx, but to me a sinister figure. He's up there like a Byzantine image of the Christ, the pantocrator, the all-ruler, soaring up as you see him in the apses of Byzantine churches.

THE TRIAL 1953–54
Oil on canvas, 72 x 63 in.
Art Institute of Chicago
(Friends of American Art, 1954.438)
© 1989 The Art Institute of Chicago

THE BANQUET 1954
Oil on canvas, 30 x 25¼ in.
Whereabouts unknown

Study for ELECTION NIGHT 1954
Oil on canvas, 24 x 21 in.
Private collection

CIGARETTE GIRL 1957
Oil on canvas, 40 x 35 in.
Sid Deutsch Gallery, New York

ELECTION NIGHT II 1954–55
Oil on canvas, 20 x 24 in.
Montgomery Museum of Fine Arts, Alabama

Commentary on
ELECTION NIGHT
ELECTION NIGHT II

My involvement with painting and with the history of it is very strong. Sean O'Casey said that an artist needs, among other things, some involvement with the art that has come before, and God knows I do. Many of my ideas are simply based on painting which has already been done. It has to be that way. I can only think in terms of something with a precedent. *Election Night* is the Last Supper—and not the *last* Last Supper, by any means. In this scene,

however, there are women present, as there almost always are at these political functions. There's a haughty matron, a tall statuesque woman in mink with large staring eyes. I was trying to arrive at the female equivalent of some of the terrible men I'd been depicting. I have some fat ladies there too, but I have never painted any of them with a bad complexion; they are always glowing.

ELECTION NIGHT 1954
Oil on canvas, 63⅛ x 72½ in.
The Museum of Modern Art, New York
Gift of Joseph H. Hirshhorn

MEDICINE SHOW 1955–56
Oil on canvas, 72 x 63 in.
Metropolitan Museum of Art

STANDING WOMAN (Study for MEDICINE SHOW)
Graphite on white paper, 15½ x 11½ in.
Fogg Art Museum, Harvard University, Cambridge, Mass.
Gift of Meta and Paul J. Sachs

◀ **Study for MEDICINE SHOW III** 1955
Oil on canvas, 16 x 14 in.
Maurice Weir

Commentary on MEDICINE SHOW series

I wanted to paint a scene out of doors, not having done one for a long time. I paint buildings rather well and like doing so. I don't want to paint the same picture over and over again. So I said to myself next: "What would draw the people together?" Something has to, and there must be people. What shall they do? A "Special on Tomatoes"? No. A street magician? Maybe. Then: how to relate women to a scene like this? The nude—for I wanted to paint a nude at this time—could be the cigarette girl. There might be call girls as well. And acrobats, posing in the direction of a maestro. So I came up with the idea of a medicine show. But it's a fantasy. I don't want to paint a real documentary of commercialism. On the other hand, all the elements of TV advertising and Madison Avenue could be here. The word *veleno* which you see on the tray the cigarette girl is carrying is the Italian word for "poison," but it is my invention as a trade name for commercialism. It could be the right title for the picture as a whole, too. I could make it much more specific as allegory or satire—but why should I? This pitchman on the platform is the true ancestor of

them all. And if I got more specific, I'd be painting things I'd never painted before and probably couldn't paint well, like a TV set, an airplane, an automobile, a billboard.

I've always tried to make some point about charlatans— in this case, a medicine show, or in some other case, somebody doing card tricks, or pulling a rabbit out of a hat. I've always been trying to make a kind of indictment of mysticism, and people being fooled, people being gulled. I don't think I ever quite brought it off. I think that in fact what I succeeded in doing in *Medicine Show* is expressing a certain nostalgia. There's a city background which is really South Boston. There is a sailor and there is a girl, and the girl wears a kind of blouse which is gathered, and there's a man with a straw hat, and all this could have happened around 1935, when I was very young. And I don't think I make the point at all about how Madison Avenue is born and all the lies they tell, which is what I planned to do.

But if you could work hypothetically: I'm going to do this and this is the subject, and if you come out with that,

it means that you followed a blueprint. And that's not what painting is all about either. You get a notion in your head, and whatever you do, whatever you come up with, that's it. And you can follow Euclid; you can say q.e.d. But in that respect it reminds me of painting a large painting which is simply an enlargement of the small one, and that's no fun. It's no fun I think to start working on a huge canvas knowing exactly what you're going to do. What's the point? So I've started out with subjects which have turned out to be something quite other. It seems like this *Medicine Show* and its brethren want to be a nostalgia painting and a city scene. I had a script and then more or less disregarded it. What richness it has may be in that procedure. But somewhere, way back, you have to have a script, or a text, and a pretty complete one. Without the challenge of plot building, mental laziness sets in. I don't like arbitrariness. I prefer a train of thought that will lead me, through its own natural requirements, to delectable paint. An art-school model or classical nude is no good for me. I need a specific psychological reason. When I said

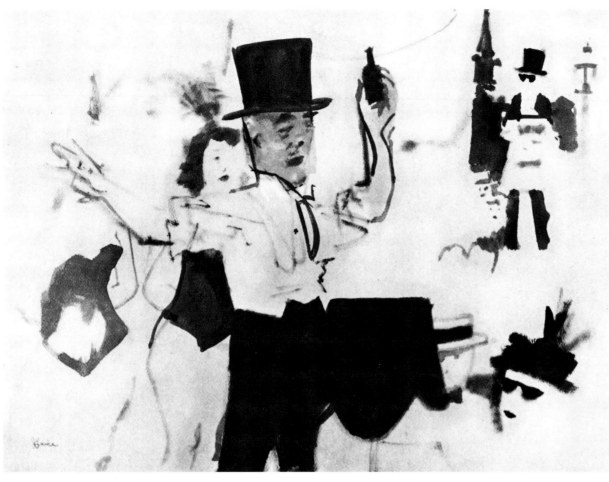

Study for MEDICINE SHOW 1954
Pencil on paper, 11 x 13¾ in.
Whereabouts unknown

MEDICINE MAN 1958
Oil and gouache on paper, 20 x 25½ in.
Whereabouts unknown

to a friend of mine who is a painter, "You can't know too much," his reply was, "You can't forget too much"—which may be a sign of the overvaluation of temperament in our day. Painters, since the First World War and maybe earlier, are supposed to be rhapsodic about themselves. But as for me, I want to remember *everything*. I'm not a primitive, or a space cadet, which is another kind of primitive, a self-conscious one—and I don't want to be. I have never learned to draw a hand well enough, so why should I stop trying now?

In the big *Medicine Show*, there is an image of a skull-like man against an intense blue sky, and something came through that was more important than my original intention. Charles Alan, who was my dealer at that time, had seen Ingmar Bergman's film *Wild Strawberries*, and he thought my painting embodied some of the same kind of nightmarish stuff—you know, "Nightmare under a Brilliant Noonday Sun." I'll settle for that.

MEDICINE SHOW I 1955
Oil on canvas, 40⅛ x 45¼ in.
The Pennsylvania Academy of the Fine Arts
Henry D. Gilpin and John Lambert Fund

MEDICINE SHOW IV 1958
Oil on canvas, 35 x 40 in.
Wichita Art Museum
Roland P. Murdock Collection

HILLEL 1955
Oil on panel, 10 x 8 in.
Whereabouts unknown

74

JUDAH 1957
Oil on panel, 10 x 8 in.
Private collection

THE SCRIBE 1956
Oil on panel, 10 x 8 in.
Hirshhorn Museum and Sculpture Garden, Smithsonian Institution
Gift of Joseph H. Hirshhorn, 1966

NEHEMIAH ca. 1958
Oil on panel, 10 x 8 in.
Susanna Levine Fisher

SUSANNA 1957
Oil on canvas, 20 x 15
Collection of the artist

I painted this as a Mother's Day present for Ruth, instead
of going to a shop uptown and buying something for her.
At that age our daughter, Susanna, wanted to be a
ballerina, and here I've painted her in the kind of dress
she wore at the time—a white pinafore with pink polka
dots—and a flower-covered plastic "tiara" in her hair.

SUSANNA AS A CHARRO 1957–89
Oil on canvas, 60 x 40 in.
Collection of the artist

A *charro* is a Mexican cowboy, and in Mexico they make
charro outfits for children. I was down there with my wife
and daughter and we bought her one, and she looked
absolutely charming in it. Little girls look better in these
things than little boys. I decided to do a painting, but as
I worked on it something went wrong, and I've been
picking at it ever since, especially since it's been hanging in my living room. By now I think I've made it better, but it certainly has accumulated a lot of paint.

PORTRAIT OF SUSANNA ca. 1958
Oil on canvas, 24 x 21 in.
Susanna Levine Fisher

Susanna was in grammar school then, and she would sometimes come to my studio on Bleecker Street after school and pose for me. She went to school in Greenwich Village, and my studio was in the same neighborhood—right above the Bleecker Street Cinema. When I painted this portrait, she was wearing a green sweater and a plaid skirt, a typical schoolgirl's outfit.

PORTRAIT OF RUTH 1957
Oil on canvas, 24 x 21 in.
Collection of the artist

Ruth had beautiful black hair at that time. We were living uptown then, on West 95th Street, and I painted this portrait in her studio, with the background full of racks of her pictures. She thought it turned out well—that it was full of life, and not unflattering (which was her main consideration). She always thought she was better-looking than she for some reason felt I thought she was.

Ruth never would have been a portrait painter herself. I think that to be a portrait painter you have to be interested in verisimilitude, even if you distort, and that was not in her. She tended toward a more abstract pictorialism, and was more involved with color relationships, pattern, and, later on, a vehemence of stroke, and always a certain psychological tension.

Commentary on
THIRTY-FIVE MINUTES FROM TIMES SQUARE
THE GIRLS FROM FLEUGEL STREET

I often paint a picture on an idea that I've done before because there don't exactly seem to be ideas flowing, and I take an old theme because I feel like I ought to produce more work than I do. Sometimes it's just the desire to paint something completely different from the thematic subjects that I've been working on, and go back to the idea of painting a nude or painting something with a lighter color or texture or a lighter idea to it, painting a face, painting a figure. I think it's the most important reason in the case of so many of these paintings, like *Thirty-five Minutes from Times Square,* or *The Girls from Fleugel Street,* or *Cigarette Girl.* They're all done as what Graham Greene once called entertainments. Except that with these I'm entertaining myself. It's something which is its own reason to do. It's pleasurable, and it's also very *Threepenny Opera* sometimes, but it becomes possible for me to enjoy myself with prismatic color and perhaps not to be so bloody meaningful, but to have a good time.

Fleugel Street is one of those mythical places that were in burlesque show dialogues. It was *the* street where the stripteaser meets the comedian. The straight one is usually the smart guy, and the comedian is usually the fall guy, and he's always getting taken. So he meets this girl who bumps her hip at him, and he goes ape. He's so mad to possess her, and of course he winds up nowhere. That's what happens on Fleugel Street.

THIRTY-FIVE MINUTES FROM TIMES SQUARE 1956
Oil on canvas, 48 x 39⅛ in.
Hirshhorn Museum and Sculpture Garden, Smithsonian Institution
Gift of Joseph H. Hirshhorn Foundation, 1966

GIRLS FROM FLEUGEL STREET 1958 ▶
Oil on canvas, 64 x 56 in.
Mr. & Mrs. Gerrit Van de Bovenkamp

LOVE, OH CARELESS LOVE 1959
Oil on canvas, 56 x 64 in.
Private collection

The title *Love, Oh Careless Love* comes from a blues song that I think was based on a melody from *Aida*. The painting features two rather seedy characters, a man and a woman, sitting at a table in a rather rundown establishment. He has no jacket on, and she is wearing a see-through blouse, a low-cut jumper, and a wilted floral hat—once more, the type of woman of questionable reputation that Lotte Lenya would play. I particularly like the lazy susan on the table, just the kind you used to see in all the cafeterias, with a mustard pot, a horseradish pot, and jars of hot sauce and ketchup with stoppers in them. The composition is carefully designed, in terms of the arrangement of darks and lights, and forms a nearly flat pattern much as *The Turnkey* does.

RECLINING NUDE 1956
Oil on canvas, 15 x 20 in.
Mrs. Oliver Baker, New York

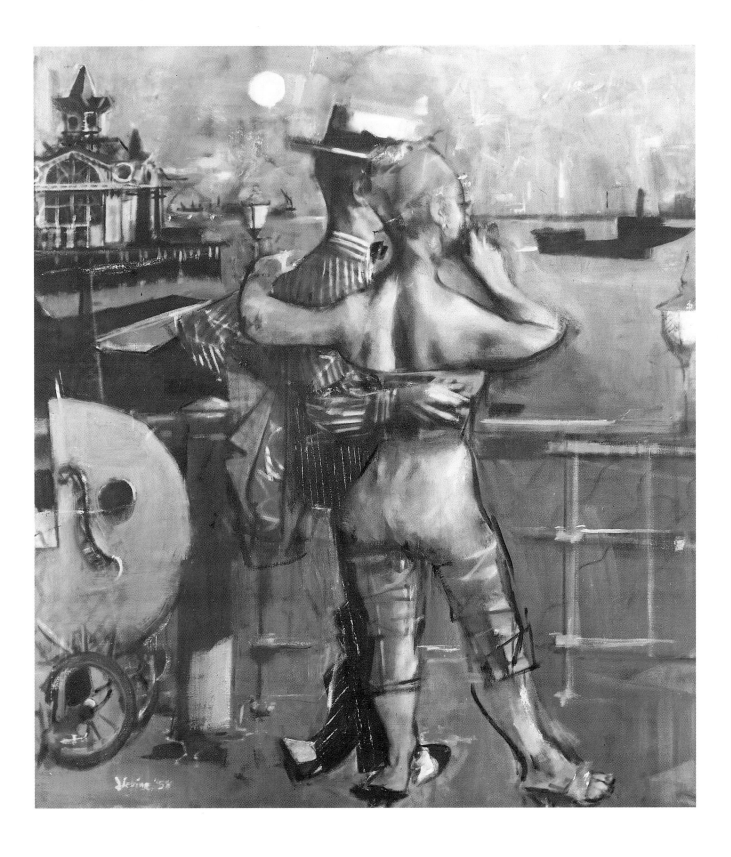

THE BLACK FREIGHTER 1958
Oil on canvas, 40 x 35 in.
Neuberger Museum
State University of New York at Purchase
Gift of Roy R. Neuberger

The Black Freighter was inspired by a song that Lotte Lenya sings in *The Threepenny Opera* about a black freighter. Here, a young couple stands near a fireboat station on the shore of the Hudson River, somewhere downtown, and watches a freighter go by. She's wearing a halter top and pedal pushers—very long short pants that were popular then—and he's wearing a striped shirt and a straw hat, and next to them is a baby carriage. The sky breaks up into something sort of Impressionist, an effect that I later reprised in *Carnival at Sunset*, 1984.

◄ INAUGURATION 1956–58
Oil on canvas, 72 x 63 in.
National Museum of American Art, Smithsonian Institution
Gift of the Sara Roby Foundation

I had done a courtroom, which you might say is the Judiciary, and I decided that I should do something on the Executive branch of the government—a picture of the Chief Executive. At that point I decided that even *I* didn't think that the President of the United States was an evil man, even if he were Eisenhower, or even, God help us, Reagan. Perhaps no Lincoln, no Jefferson, no Washington, but not an evil-meaning man. For the purposes of drama, I fixed on a character who was like a composite of several presidents I didn't care for—I think mostly Harry Truman and Woodrow Wilson, two men who were presumably righteous but to me really unlovable. In an inauguration, all of the important personages are in profile, and someone like a chief clerk is full face and seems to dominate all the proceedings, although he doesn't matter at all. Dramatically, this is really silly, and it really became silly in Reagan's second inauguration, when the figure in full face was Nancy Reagan, who was *really* meaningless. However, perhaps someday I'll do a tailpiece to this and I'll have the Chief Justice and the President and a tiny aging lady in a little red pillbox hat. That will really be a silly thing.

INAUGURATION II 1958
Oil on canvas, 32 x 28 in.
Whereabouts unknown

THE SENATOR 1958
Oil on canvas, 35 x 40 in.
Mr. & Mrs. Gerrit Van de Bovenkamp

Raphael Soyer once said that I had gestures in my paintings that nobody ever did and that nobody *can* do—I suppose because I made most of them up. This senator is a pompous windbag, extending his left hand in an odd oratorical flourish. The painting relates closely in size and in focus to *The Judge*, 1953, although the foreshortening is more extreme and it is not quite as atmospheric or as richly painted. *The Senator* is a rather hard-working study of a solid enclosed in a prism, and I tried to account for every inch of depth, to create a structure where you could tell exactly where you were within every point of that shallow space.

THE TURNKEY 1956
Oil on canvas, 54 x 60⅛ in.
Hirshhorn Museum and Sculpture Garden, Smithsonian Institution
Gift of Joseph H. Hirshhorn Foundation, 1966

◄ *The Turnkey* is an essay in what I think a fat little corseted general in Franco's Spain might have been like. It's a very nearly flat pattern painting, with dominant dark shapes of burnt umber—not shadows, but what the Japanese call *notan* (color value)—on an ecru background, with sudden shots of color. I was thinking of the Tosa school of Japanese painting.

I took great relish in painting the still life on the general's desk: a small freestanding clock, a cracked egg in an eggcup, an address book, a lady's fan, a garter, a desk blotter, and a lot of rubber stamps. And in the background there's a prie-dieu, part of a crucifix, and an arched window with bars on it opening onto the prison (which I filched from Goya). And I introduced what I considered to be the ultimate in vulgarity—a Tiffany lampshade. There were none to be found at that time; I believe that some tycoon, a merchandizer, had an enormous cache of them in storage, and there were none available. So I invented one.

1932 (IN MEMORY OF GEORGE GROSZ) 1959
Oil on canvas, 56 x 49 in.
Mr. & Mrs. Robert M. Topol

I think that an artist should paint his life, and I try to, and I am a social painter to the degree that the society or the body politic impinges on my life. The gas ovens were too horrible for me to face. Now Hitler and Hindenburg—that was an aspect I *could* face. Somebody showed me a book about Germany, and a line caught my eye about Hindenburg being a giant of a man, and that set me off. I also recalled seeing a photograph by Erich Salomon showing him in the front row of an opera house, seated between the king of Egypt and a large female opera singer. His head was enormous, like a huge projectile.

In my painting, the senile, stupid figure of President Hindenburg is handing over the baton of power to Hitler, a creepy little man with an expression like the face of a shark. It's the only time I ever painted an image as silly as Hitler; it could be a Disney character. Hannah Arendt's phrase "the banality of evil" applies here. The figure on the left behind Hindenburg, rubbing his hands together in anticipation, could be Franz von Papen, who was instrumental in this particular chapter of Hitler's rise to power; but I might also have been thinking of the wonderful German actor and director Erich von Stroheim. After

all, what you don't see in the newspapers, you might see in the movies. I painted the background as a military museum. Up on a pedestal right behind Hindenburg is an equestrian figure in full armor, including an emblazoned shield, and the windows are Gothic.

The title was really an afterthought. George Grosz, who is one of the few 20th-century artists I admire, had just died; and, as he had frequently chosen to attack the perversity of German fascism through his art, I thought it would be a fitting tribute.

FÊTES GALANTES 1959
Oil on canvas, 49 x 56 in.
Mr. & Mrs David Pincus

Fêtes Galantes is in a way a reprise of *Election Night*, but without politicians. It's just a nightclub full of people who are well-off, with a cigarette girl in top hat in the foreground on the left and a group of musicians behind her— an accordionist, a guitarist, and a gypsy violinist. I myself wouldn't be able to bear that gypsy violin in my ear while I was eating. The painting is quite rich in color and rhapsodic, even if it's no formal breakthrough. It's a romance.

above left:

THE PINK HAT 1957
Oil on canvas, 25 x 18 in.
Private collection

LADY WITH OPERA GLASSES 1959
Oil on canvas, 14 x 12 in.
Private collection

Degas was fascinated by women with opera glasses, so I couldn't have painted this without thinking of him. (I also included one in *On the Block*, the painting I'm doing now.) I'm particularly happy with the formal composition of *Lady with Opera Glasses*, which is an essay in rounds and half-rounds: the lady's round face and round bodice, and her semi-circular hat, cut off by the top edge of the canvas; and the oculus at the left and the dome's curving base at the right. This sense of roundness comes across in depth as well as on the surface. And I achieved an arabesque of lights and darks in the process, which gives it both good design and a dramatic effect.

GIRL IN ORANGE 1959
Oil on canvas, 20 x 16 in.
Whereabouts unknown

In *Oak Street*, there's a lanky, raw-boned figure of a derelict next to the window of a pawnshop. I hadn't used this sort of considerable elongation for some time. I was inspired to paint this figure by a character in Brecht's *Threepenny Novel*, Fewkoombey, who is a veteran of the Boer War and is now a tattered beggar practically incapable of speech. I called it *Oak Street* perhaps because Old Oak Street was the location of Peachum's headquarters in the novel.

THREE GRACES 1959
Oil on canvas, 21 x 24 in.
Midtown Galleries, New York

Like Rubens, I love to paint flesh. Adjectives like lambent, corruscating, iridescent, glowing—that is what I am after. I want to incorporate the nude into my work. I want to, even though I am a satirist and even though I sometimes feel like sermonizing, because I see no harm in having an attractive body in there once in a while. So I worked out an iconography which might be "The Three Graces." It might be "The Judgment of Paris." When you paint the female figure without a model, you're seeing and not seeing. But I am not the kind of artist that makes a Greek amphora, and while I admire the airfoil wing of a plane, I am not so much for these long, extended lines. The long-legged *Harper's Bazaar* model isn't really my thing, and so my figures are apt to be a little dumpy and a little clumsy, and moreover, that's the human body as I *do* it. I see it as everyone else sees it, but I don't *do* what I see. Physiognomists, never do as much with the body as they do with the head. This is true of people like Rembrandt or even Daumier, and in my small way, I think I'm like that too.

91

אדם

חוה

This *Adam and Eve* is quite a bit larger than the *Adam and Eve* I'd painted in 1951 or any of the other biblical scenes of Hebraica I'd done, which had always been quite small—about 8 by 10 inches—and which were in that sense modest. But I started thinking of Adam and Eve in a larger sense. You're painting the female body and the male body, and it's a sally into the painting of the physicality of the human race. Can it be said that that's religious? I remember a hilarious experience Ruth and I had. We were in the Sistine Chapel, and there was a Roman guide with a lot of Americans in tow. He was pointing out the meaning of the different tableaux, and he said, "Up there is Adam—you've heard of him, of course." What I mean is you can't exactly say it's religious. It's the general concept of the beginning of humanity. It's also anatomical. Also—if I don't do something like *Adam and Eve*, I am either reduced to the model sitting in the studio like a dummy, or, Lord help us, pornography! If you want to paint the human body, and you want to use it in some sort of context, there isn't much in the contemporary world—well, beach scenes, people with bikinis. But that is not dramatically or emotionally very satisfying. Adam and Eve is a great excuse to paint the human body, of both sexes. In terms of precedents I might have had in mind in this instance, there is a painting by Titian of Adam and Eve which Rubens did a free copy of, although when it comes to the Adam, I seem to be a little bit more obsessed with El Greco than Titian or Rubens or anyone else. As for Eve, I don't know. She's a bit more mysterious.

The '6Os

Art with a social message had been *de rigueur* in the '30s. I knew it was considered passé by the '60s, but I felt that I had a personal commitment to sustain it and to come up with topics I felt I needed to do. I think it often resulted in a certain dryness and a certain lack of thrust or motivation that couldn't be helped, for the times were against it. But I went on doing it anyway because I always feel like bucking the times, whatever they are. And it often led to my reprising a lot of themes instead of finding some new direction. But I was of a certain age and a certain time, and I went with what I had to go on. Sometimes I had a felicitous period when I had a piece of something that I enjoyed working on. This wasn't always the case, and I really couldn't make common cause with the kids of the '60s. I was of parental age, and I had my own tradition. Besides, I wasn't crazy about those kids or their aesthetic, even if I sympathized with some of their politics. Everything seemed to be homemade with them. They'd flog a guitar or draw or paint as they learn to do in progressive school, and there was no sense of any craft or high form; their artistic expression was on the same level as their denim pants. I have very little respect for that. My daughter is about that age, and I often felt like I had to rescue her for Mozart, to help her find her way out of the herd. It's the vulgarities that society sets up that's an impediment. I believe that if you like shoddy dance music and cheap Broadway tunes, then you can't really have an ear for late Beethoven. I don't think it's possible to have an appreciation for both. That's the way I see it. I'm peculiar that way. I don't know anyone who reacts as I do. I'm not a snob. It's just that I think it was an effort to get here, and all that stuff was just so many stumbling blocks. I was a friend of Leonard Bernstein before the war. One time he got absolutely obsessed with a song called "Tangerine" and would burst into singing it at the oddest times. Well, when it comes to knowledgeability about music I certainly defer to him. But somehow or other I was not about to sing "Tangerine" myself.

I visited Israel for the first time in 1962. Although this trip did not have an immediate effect on my work—in the sense that it did not result in any paintings—I was affected enough by my visit to want to return, which I did with Ruth in the '70s, and again since then. On this first trip I went alone, a guest of the American Jewish Congress at a symposium on Israeli culture and its American counterparts. I was one of several American cultural figures who'd been invited, including the composer Marc Blitzstein and the producer Harold Prince. In the course of my small contribution to this dialogue, I made the following remarks: "As America was going into the Depression, I began to realize the rich, full tradition in the labor movement that the Jews had had in terms of liberal and progressive thought, and I became involved with that. Furthermore, I began, in a dim way, to think in terms of a sort of humanism, which I believe, which I understand, has its Jewish, Hebraic antecedents....As for being a Jewish painter, I don't know. I've been a political-social painter, for the most part a satirist. I think I have tried to express, in my work, some sort of an ethic which may stem from some of our traditions, but it is not necessarily turned back within the Jewish community. I try to paint for everybody and anybody that will look, and consequently it hasn't been an introverted expression, let's say, in the ethnic sense. But there's no question in my mind that after some fashion, I'm true to my tradition, and to my teaching."

THE BOY DAVID PLAYING THE HARP 1960
Oil on canvas, 16 x 14 in.
Matthew A. Meyer, New York

Friends of mine, the Matthew Meyers, asked me to do a painting, and this was the result. I believe it was a birthday present for Matthew from his wife, and, as I recall, the theme was suggested by them. It's the biblical figure David as a little boy, done the way Donatello or Desiderio da Settigano might have painted him.

THE PRINCESS 1960
Oil on canvas, 78 x 48 in.
Mr. & Mrs. Gerrit Van de Bovenkamp

The Princess was an effort at a formal portrait. I originally had it in mind to do Grace Kelly, when she became a princess, but she's too beautiful for parody. If you try to do a parody of a woman like that, it won't look like her. Well, I did my best and finally I just wound up painting my idea of a Velázquez or a Gainsborough or something like that. It's a society portrait. When I was a kid, I once thought I might be a society portrait painter, but unfortunately nobody in Boston wanted me. I don't think I would have remained a portrait painter, but I certainly love the great portrait paintings, the Holbeins and the Van Dykes. It's generally thought that that cannot be done anymore—that you can't do a commissioned portrait that will please your customer *and* create a work of art. That's another 20th-century premise I don't accept. I think it's possible.

94

THE LAST WALTZ 1962
Oil on canvas, 78 x 48 in.
Hirshhorn Museum and Sculpture Garden
Smithsonian Institution
Gift of Joseph H. Hirshhorn, 1966

The Last Waltz is sort of formal. I had in mind a man who
might be a senior State Department official, dancing with
a very young girl who might suggest in some way the
tenderness and vulnerability of the world that was in his
hands. I don't think I really made the point though. I
based the man's head partly on my memory of the head of
a man in an El Greco portrait and partly on the movie
actor John Boles.

There's an interesting anecdote connected with *The Last
Waltz*. I knew a lawyer, quite a few years back, who owned
two very good Soutines that he allowed me to come and see.
He had a daughter who was interested in modern art, and
she happened to see *The Last Waltz*, and a short time later
I met her on the street. She reproached me for having
repudiated the modernist movement, which I happily
accepted, because I don't mean to be a part of that anyway.
This girl married an English duke, and became a duchess,
and I keep weighing in my mind, which is the greater
apostasy, hers or mine? She disowned the Consititution of
the United States, and I have only gone my own way,
disregarding things that are supposed to be incumbent on
me but which I refuse to accept.

Young people had just begun to sit in coffee houses in New York, and the Figaro, at Bleecker and Macdougal streets, was a new place to hang out. They liked to act like they were poor and gifted. And they were neither one nor the other. Although I based the figures in these paintings on observation, I made them up. In *Café Figaro*, there's a long-haired girl smoking a cigarette at a sidewalk table with a beared young man full of bravado, who is wearing dark glasses and a striped shirt; and in the foreground to their right is a namby-pamby-looking girl who could have just as easily been in one of John Sloan's paintings from the '40s. I suppose they fancied themselves to be the new "lost generation."

Café is one of those paintings I did just to do. Actually, it's a harmony in orange and green. I'm not Whistler, but every now and then I get obsessed by a certain harmony, and I'll paint a picture for that reason. And the subject might just be a device.

CAFÉ 1960
Oil on canvas, 42 x 48 in.
Maier Museum of Art, Randolph-Macon
Women's College, Lynchburg, Va.

below left:
BEATNIK GIRL 1959
Oil on canvas, 28 x 21 in.
Private collection
Mr. & Mrs. Michael Erlinger

CAFÉ FIGARO 1960
Oil on canvas, 21 x 24 in.
Dr. & Mrs. J. B. Yasinow, Philadelphia

The early '60s was not much of a political period in my work. I had had a large show at the Alan Gallery, and Alan advised me at that time to paint some portraits and not worry about subject matter for a while, and I took his advice. It was a kind of dry spell for me as far as themes are concerned, and it seemed like I could relax by getting a model and just painting, painting something three-dimensional and focal in front of me. I don't need a model, in the sense that I don't depend on the reality in front of me to paint the human figure. However, one develops what Gombrich calls *schemata*—mental images of the figure—which can become pretty complete by my age, but, at the same token, can also become somewhat arid and clichéd. A model can give you a fresh look and cause you to paint something you wouldn't otherwise have done. So I began to get models to come in. My studio was so filthy that it was too much to ask them to take their clothes off, so I just did portraits of them.

I did do some nudes at that time, and a few paintings of partially dressed women in brothel settings— a kind of woman as sex symbol who is no beauty—but these were all done without models. In *Blue Angel*, a prostitute is sitting in a bedroomy corner with a rose-colored lampshade and a water pitcher. She's half-dressed and looks very angry, not because I want to say that this is an evil, but simply that she's an angry girl who isn't being given a very fair shake. My wife, who was quite a feminist in her own idiosyncratic way, once complimented me on seeing it that way, instead of the cliché way of the woman standing under the lamp post, with one knee advanced. That is one of the clichés of our time, like "moon in June." I saw it more like the brothel scene in *Threepenny Opera*, with Lotte Lenya as Jenny. You can identify with her in some way. You don't even know Lenya, but it gets to you. With Degas's depictions of laundresses and prostitutes, you don't identify with them. They are searing and acutely observed, but they don't bond you in any way. For all his greatness, that's not what he does. I'm not the first person to say that. Van Gogh surmised that Degas never completed the sexual act, and it's the same way with his work.

I was in a brothel once, in Brazil during the war. I was on a troop ship in the army and we stopped at Recife, and I went with a gang of guys off the ship. But it was very off-putting, and I certainly couldn't go through with it.

THE GREEN CLOCHE 1962
Oil on canvas, 24 x 21 in.
Hirshhorn Museum and Sculpture Garden,
Smithsonian Institution
Gift of Joseph H. Hirshhorn, 1966

BEDROOM SCENE 1961
Oil on canvas, 20 x 16 in.
Private collection

BLUE ANGEL 1961
Oil on canvas, 26 x 32 in.
Mary Bert & Alvin P. Gutman

BIRMINGHAM '63 1963
Oil on canvas, 71 x 75½ n.
Marjorie and Charles Benton Collection, Evanston, Illinois

WITCHES' SABBATH 1963
Oil on canvas, 96 x 84 in.
Benton Foundation, Chicago, Illinois

◄ *Commentary on* **BIRMINGHAM '63**

A guy I used to see around, a dispatcher for the *Nation* or the *New Republic*, I think, used to tell me I should paint something about race relations in the South, about what was going on down there at that time. And once I said to him, "Don't bug me. Art is emotion recollected in tranquility. Let me alone, for chrissakes." But I found myself starting a painting, immediately after, on just that theme. I had seen a picture in the newspapers of a dog snarling and snapping at a group of blacks, and I had an image like that in my mind when I began painting *Birmingham*.

◄ *Commentary on* **WITCHES' SABBATH**

To be trenchant at all as a satirist, one would have to find topics which, though universal, permit a state of alienation, as today's catchword goes. I had painted the courts and had felt there was enough good to be said for them to render me irresolute; I had painted a presidential inauguration and found it impossible to think of an American president in my lifetime of whom nothing good could be said. I was becoming the first social commentator in paint who didn't know how he felt.

I kept thinking that somewhere in the legislative branch of government lay my opportunity. The idea began with a simple format—a committee around a table. It developed rapidly into a barnyard with a goat, a pig, and chickens on the one hand; and on the other a pageant of American folk regalia, a Shriner, a Legionnaire, a Klansman, a cowboy, a member of the Ancients and Honourables. Now I felt I was free-associating, as they say. I dropped the pig, the chickens became pigeons, an ape playing with documents on the table was discarded. I was hindered by indecision about a witness (friendly or not?). The barnyard suggested a pumpkin. Hallowe'en suggested Witches' Sabbath. I dropped the witness, added an old typewriter, and I was in business.

THE ART LOVER 1962
Oil on canvas, 56⅛ x 49 in.
National Museum of American Art,
Smithsonian Institution
Gift of S.C. Johnson and Son, Inc.

From time to time I get the urge to lampoon the art world. Here I've portrayed an aesthete as a mock figure of royalty. I had seen a French engraving of a king and queen from about the 17th century, and I did a couple of paintings based on it. I still have the canvas with the queen left in; it could be a companion piece.

RECONSTRUCTION 1963
Oil on canvas, 35 x 40 in.
Private collection

Reconstruction is about Germany being reconstructed after the war. I painted a man who was my idea of a kind of German prototype, kind of corpulent, with small features. And he is surrounded with the paraphernalia of his business—a pair of scales, an hourglass, and in the back, through a window, as it were, a huge orange earth mover. I was doing something like Holbein's portrait of Georg Gisze, a merchant, with all the instruments of his profession.

THE SPANISH PRISON 1959–62
Oil on canvas, 28 x 32 in.
Mr. & Mrs. Peter Blum

The Spanish Prison is my notion of a prison scene in
Franco's Spain. The prisoner has a white gag around the
lower part of his face, and, in a simple visual reversal, the
executioner is wearing a black mask and the kind of black
patent-leather hat worn by the Spanish police. This visual
counterpoint, with the mouth of one covered in white and
the eyes of the other covered in black, vividly conveys the
awful contrast and inequality of their positions. The
prisoner is the victim, gagged to prevent him from expressing his viewpoint, while the mask preserves his oppressor's
anonymity.

THE JUDGMENT OF PARIS (Paris as a Greenwich Village Dreamer) 1964
Oil on canvas, 54 x 64 in.
Marjorie and Charles Benton Collection, Chicago, Illinois

Commentary on JUDGMENT OF PARIS series

I painted a series of canvases on the theme of the Judgment of Paris, each time using a different composition and a different approach. In the first one I didn't even include Paris—it's just two nude women and a woman in a dress, sort of a frontal Three Graces. The second one is more elaborate, with Mercury and Paris and the three goddesses, all more or less nude. It's kind of a stuffed canvas with five people. I have the Expressionists' horror of a vacuum, which I have to rescue myself from one day and leave a large blank area on a canvas.

In *Judgment of Paris III*, Paris is wearing a little beret and smoking a cigar, and looking a little bit like Lautrec, and the goddesses are wearing stockings (two of them with garters and corsets, the other one nothing else). I turned *Judgment of Paris IV* into a house of fashion, with one tall model posing, and another being fitted, and Paris as the designer with a big pair of shears, and there's also a dressmaker and a camera man. So that's the rag trade—a different kind of Judgment of Paris. In the fifth one, Paris is seated and in front of him are the three goddesses, as if on a stage: I've done Venus to look like Marlene Dietrich in *The Blue Angel*, and I've made Juno an opera singer with a huge bosom; and I've painted Minerva as a warrior-maiden with a helmet and a spear. But I've done Paris as a self-portrait—myself when I was younger, obviously. All the figures are clothed in that one. In *Judgment of Paris VI*, which is the last, they're all nude again, except for the Tanagra hats that the three goddesses are wearing.

I don't remember what my motivation was to paint these, except the usual one: it is an excuse to paint the nude. I'm looking for excuses to paint all the time, really. I'm trying to reward myself with interesting possibilities, because the thing to fight is boredom.

THE JUDGMENT OF PARIS II 1964
Oil on canvas, 21 x24 in.
Philip Sills

Study for JUDGMENT OF PARIS 1963
Brush and ink on paper, 11 x 15½ in.
Philip Sills
▼

THE JUDGMENT OF PARIS I 1964
Oil on canvas, 32 x 26 in.
Private collection

**THE JUDGMENT OF PARIS III (Paris as a
   Movie Director)** 1964
Oil on canvas, 26 x 32 in.
Marjorie and Charles Benton Collection
Evanston, Illinois

**THE JUDGMENT OF PARIS IV (Paris Wearing
   a Phrygian Cap)** 1964
Oil on canvas, 26 x 32 in.
Marjorie and Charles Benton Collection
Evanston, Illinois

THE JUDGMENT OF PARIS V (The Artist as Himself as Paris) 1964
Oil on canvas, 26 x 32 in.
Marjorie and Charles Benton Collection
Evanston, Illinois

THE JUDGMENT OF PARIS VI (Paris as a Fashion Photographer) 1964
Oil on canvas, 26 x 32 in.
Marjorie and Charles Benton Collection
Evanston, Illinois

THE GREAT SOCIETY 1967
Oil on canvas, 63 x 56 in.
Midtown Galleries, New York

Commentary on
THE ROARING TROPICS

Ruth and I had gone down to Puerto Rico and stayed at a hotel there. It was filled with American tourists, almost all of whom fit the classic stereotype: fleshy women, and cigar-smoking men with huge bellies. Actually, the women weren't nearly as bad as the men. *The Roaring Tropics* was an effort on my part to do the human figure again, even if a touch on the Rabelaisian and Gargantuan side. It's all flesh, anatomy, and color. I thought it had beautiful possibilities, because with bikini bathing suits there are little shots of color interspersed among the areas of flesh, and then you get a little triangle of fabric that can be floral, or a bright solid color like magenta or cerise. There are very few subjects that give you that latitude of combining bodies with geometric shapes and colors such as the triangles and lozenges of the bikinis. You can practically make music with them. It's a real Renaissance challenge. I did things in *The Roaring Tropics* that I had never done before, such as the involved drawing and painting coloration in the middle distance, so I'm pleased with it from that standpoint.

I don't read *The New York Times* anymore—I think that three branches of government are enough—but I read the tabloids, and I invariably read the gossip columns that they print. And I had read about the black-and-white ball that Truman Capote had organized at the Plaza, which is what set me off here. It was one of those trendy society events that attracts a certain crowd—you can see a couple of young women in Mary Quant dresses, and among the recognizable celebrities I had in mind, in addition to Capote (at the far right), there was Allen Ginsberg, the bearded man at the left. For the title of the painting, I borrowed President Lyndon Johnson's phrase "The Great Society" (which is what he called his program of social improvement and noblesse oblige) and I used it ironically, doing a few of my set pieces on "the beautiful people" indulging themselves. My target was the rich rich having these very posh parties, often ostensibly for some good cause, but I think I could have done an even better job of lampooning them. I believe that there is much more I could say to put a pin through the whole trashy business, something more definitive, so that society people wouldn't dare show their faces at events like this again.

MAN WITH CIGAR 1966
Oil on canvas, 39 x 35 in.
Dr. & Mrs. Jacob Mandel

THE ROARING TROPICS 1966–69
Oil on canvas, 72 x 78 in.
Midtown Galleries, New York

SIX MASTERS: A DEVOTION 1963
Oil on canvas, 49 x 56 in.
Mr. & Mrs. Arthur J. Steel, New York

Here, I am paying homage to the six Old Masters whose work I especially love and who have influenced me the most: Rembrandt, Titian, Rubens, Goya, Velázquez, and El Greco. I should probably have put Franz Hals in there too. Basically what I am is a corporate portrait painter—by that I mean painting groups of people in hierarchies and interactions. When was the last time you ever saw a corporate portrait? The last one I can think of was by Fantin-Latour, which is not very good. You have to go back to Goya, and then back another hundred years or so to Rembrandt, Hals, and artists like them. I have always tried to learn how to paint, but most of the time I haven't felt satisfied with my means or anybody else's around me, and I've always tried to educate myself in these areas. If you want to do what was done so wonderfully by Rembrandt or Hals or Van der Helst, they're the experts on that. There's no point in trying to paint a portrait group like Raoul Dufy now, is there? So you have to learn how the masters did this, to give a decent reading of a human being, which nobody in the 20th century is particularly good at, except Kokoschka in his early work, and perhaps Graham Sutherland.

A painter once said to me that we're going to have a thousand years of nonrepresentational painting. Nonrepresentational painting is only an expression of the specialization and inhumanity of our time. It's quite possible that people will become less specialized, more human, and that the merely decorative, taken out of context, will bore them. The problem of being an artist is a problem of the pursuit of real knowledge and freedom. The mature Rembrandt was in pursuit of things that had never been tried or done before—and without his complete mastery of the tradition, his successful pursuit of them would never have been possible. So also with Titian, who grew out of Giovanni Bellini; and of all great pioneers. It is the fact that Picasso could draw like no other artist since Leonardo—his tradition-developed equipment—that is his saving grace and the thing that he will be remembered for. *Not* the fact that he invented Cubism and other gadgets.

TITIAN MISREMEMBERED 1961
Oil on canvas, 21⅛ x 24 in.
Midtown Galleries, New York

Titian Misremembered is a foolish exercise in memory, a sort of send-up of Titian's great *Rape of Europa* in Boston. I had tried to do a small version of the painting from memory, without looking at reproductions. After I compared what I had done with a reproduction, I realized that I had one angel flying down and Titian's is up, and the bull is going up and mine is going down. So I called it *Titian Misremembered*, because everything is different. Everything is literally misremembered.

DALEY'S GESTURE ca. 1969
Oil on canvas, 27½ x 31½ in.
Mr. & Mrs. Peter Blum

In the fall of 1968, *Time* Magazine invited me to go as a correspondent to the Democratic National Convention in Chicago, commissioning me to do a series of sketches as an artist's view of the activities. Many of these drawings were reproduced by *Time*, and I later used some of them as the basis for paintings and prints. One of those paintings was *Daley's Gesture*. The title refers to an incident that occurred at the convention on the night the antiwar protestors were attacked by the Chicago police on the streets outside the convention hall. Sen. Abraham Ribicoff had been outside and had seen the turmoil going on out there, with the police brutalizing the kids that were protesting, and had gone up to the podium and had just begun speaking into the mike when Daley made this "cutting the throat" gesture as a signal to his minions to cut the sound off from the senator's microphone.

I felt that I'd invented Mayor Daley as a character back in the '30s and was reassured that the type was still around. At a certain time in your life your works become historical documents which refer to an earlier period. You have to adjust from time to time. Naturally, I have adjusted, or I wouldn't be able to talk about it. At one time, I really began to be quite worried, because the idea of a tycoon of industry, if I were to paint him today, would have to a be lean, tanned, youngish-looking man with white hair, looking like certain movie actors. He would need a Mies van der Rohe setting with long lines of tubular lighting, which I would be revolted to have to paint. And he'd be wearing something like a Brooks Brothers suit, except it would be tailor-made, and I couldn't indicate the difference The nearest I came to it was in *Texas Delegate*.

I saw this delegate from the Texas contingent, and he was sprawled out on three or four folding chairs. He was quite a handsome, athletic-looking man, a real all-American hero type, much like the great ballplayer Ted Williams. but he was also very menacing-looking, as mean as a snake. And this is to me what a tycoon looks like today. As a painting, it was a challenge in terms of format—color and composition—because it's all in that shade of terra-cotta, with occasional shots of blue in the word "TEXAS" on the backs of the chairs, and I broke that up into two syllables, one on either side of the figure.

I had never done anything like the *Time* Magazine commission before, and I never did it again. I described it as "taking the King's shilling." I never felt it was right for an artist to put his talents at Henry Luce's disposal. I'd been prim about it. I never saw eye-to-eye with Ben Shahn, who I believe worked for CBS, because I have this archaic notion of what an artist's role is, and it has nothing to do with mass media, and it has nothing do with lubricating the movement of commodities. I saw the artist as being completely outside the culture… presumably like a fossil, a relic. To this day, I think of a communication in art as a communication *backwards*, to the past.

TEXAS DELEGATE 1968–71
Oil on canvas, 56 x 64 in.
Mr. & Mrs. Roger Freedman

109

The '70s

In the 1970s I was in my late 50s and early 60s, and I had pretty much established who I was as a painter and what my themes were. The 1960s ended sometime in the early '70s and kids weren't very rebellious anymore, probably because the government had stopped drafting them into the armed forces. And I was more quiescent too, although I still found a few political themes that engaged me. I only paint political paintings when I have a reason to, when my compulsion to do it gets very strong. I made quite a splash in the art world in the 1930s when I was just a kid. And it seems to me that every year since, I have become less and less well-known. I made a splash then because of a certain vehemence I had when I looked at society. I was very bitter about injustices, and I expressed a social outlook, which by the 1950s was a very unpopular thing to do. Looking back on the '70s, it seems to me as if that political motivation—that desire to satirize, to tweak the noses of the powers that be—had died in me. But when I actually look at the work I did then, I realize that I was doing as much painting of that kind as I had ever done, even though other artists I knew were not bothering with it anymore. I was alone at the old stand.

In 1972 I took my second trip to Israel, this time bringing my wife with me, and I began once again to do paintings on Old Testament themes and other Hebraica. These works were larger in scale now, because I considered them more relevant to *me*—more as personal expressions of my identity. I realized that I had been involved in too many political causes that, in the last analysis, had nothing to offer the Jews, and that when it came to the Jews the Soviet Union was a prison and Israel was one of the few places on earth where a Jew could consolidate himself. I found myself feeling a strong involvement with ancient Jewish civilization, and I began subscribing to *Biblical Archaeology* magazine.

SELF-PORTRAIT AT WESTCHESTER PARTY 1971
Oil on canvas, 41 x 47 in.
Private collection

This is a little tableau with a full-length self-portrait in the middle of it. I've painted myself in profile standing in the midst of a group of people at a party in someone's living room, and some well-to-do ladies are making a fuss over me. I'm doing a kind of shuffle, shifting my feet uneasily, and you can imagine me saying "Aw shucks, ma'am" at that very moment. Nearby there's a man who's very jovial, and very pleased with me. Everybody likes me very much, and I don't know what the hell to do, and I wish I were elsewhere.

OPENING NIGHT—MAN IN TOP HAT 1970
Oil on canvas, 24 x 21 in.
Mr. & Mrs. Jerome Westheimer, Ardmore, Okla.

OPENING NIGHT—WOMAN WITH FAN 1971
Oil on canvas, 24 x 21 in.
Private collection

◄ One of these two *Opening Night*s features an elegantly dressed woman holding a fan. What I am doing is not too far removed from writing a one-act play. Every actor needs a little business, something to do. with the hands, and a fan is a natural. The other *Opening Night* is a study of the head of a distinguished-looking man in a top hat, one of the figures in *For the Sake of Art*.

FOR THE SAKE OF ART —AVANT GARDE 1969 – 71
Oil on canvas, 78 x 72 in.
David and Rhoda Chase

For the Sake of Art depicts a number of people coming from the opera house at Lincoln Center in New York. They are very enlightened by what they saw and heard and I am glad for them. There's a limo right behind them. The little Napoleonic figure in sunglasses might be Henry Geldzahler.

STALINGRAD (The Age of Steel) ca. 1970
Oil on canvas, 72 x 64 in.
Private collection

Just after World War II, the British government had struck off a huge ceremonial sword called "The Sword of Stalingrad" as a gift from the British people to the people of Stalingrad in commemoration of the gigantic victory which turned back the Nazis. This was presented by the British ambassador to Marshal Stalin, who raised the great sword with both hands and kissed the steel blade. (Stalin means steel in Russian.) It was all in *The New York Times*.

Stalin was of course the head of state of the USSR. He was also considered by many the leading Marxist theorist and expounder. I can't think of Einstein kissing swords. The field gun in back suggests a military museum.

HONG KONG TAILOR 1970
Oil on canvas, 39 x 35 in.
Private collection

This is a painting of a very fat guy getting measured for a suit, an incident that I actually saw in Hong Kong and tried to put down in paint. I was in Hong Kong with my wife, and I went to Jack Chen's, a tailor, to get measured for some clothes. And while I was there, I saw this fat guy from New York who was being measured for his wedding suit, and he was talking very loudly to the tailor about how he's been divorced from his wife and he was marrying a Chinese girl in Hong Kong, I think, a girl who would do exactly what he wanted. When I got back to the hotel, I told Ruth about it, because it was a funny scene. Then we went to Thailand and Cambodia for a week—I believe we were just about the last American tourists to get into Cambodia—and when we were on our way back to the States, we changed planes at Hong Kong airport. Ruth spotted the fat American and his tiny Chinese bride running for their plane; she recognized them from my description. I suppose they were going on their honeymoon.

OUR PRESENCE IN THE FAR EAST 1970–71
Oil on canvas, 64 x 56 in.
Private collection

L'INDIFFÉRENT 1972
Oil on canvas, 24 x 21 in.
Jules & Connie Kay

This is really the only painting I did about Vietnam. At the left is a man who might be a professor, or he might be a general without any insignia of his rank, but he's a picture of consternation and confusion, whatever his actual position. And just behind him, to the right, is a pregnant Oriental woman whom I first imagined as a Vietnamese peasant, but she became a Chinese princess, the Imperial East. I like the ambiguity that you can't tell a general from a Columbia professor and that he doesn't know what the hell he's doing. And if the Oriental woman is pregnant, at least it represents some kind of potential. The general, the West, has no potential, just nothing. So I have myself an idea here, a haiku of an idea, maybe. However, several years after I painted this, Cambodia and Vietnam began beating the hell out of each other, and I didn't know what I thought anymore.

There's a Watteau painting, *L'Indifférent*, and this is my Watteau. This dashing young man doesn't care for the young woman, and he never will. I've painted them at a party, and it also shows that lamentable tendency that was current then for some men to unbutton their shirts all the way down to the navel and to go to parties in denim.

WOMAN OF SINT OLAFSTRAAT 1972
Oil on canvas, 40 x 35 in.
Collection of the artist

Woman of Sint Olafstraat started out as a painting of a model, but I wasn't happy with the way it was going, so I turned it into something else. The figure became a drayhorse sort of woman in an Amsterdam setting. I've been to Amsterdam frequently to look at the Rembrandts in the Rijksmuseum. Sint Olafstraat is a street in the seediest, most rundown part of Amsterdam's red-light district; it runs right behind Sint Olaf's, a Catholic church that you can see from the railroad station. Although I'm still not completely happy with the figure—I think the body is a bit misconceived—I like the sudden shots of color that I added to the overall opalescent, Old-Masterish tonality: the bright turquoise eyelid, the vermilion lipstick, and the flaming orange hairband.

DANSE CHAMPÊTRE 1975
Oil on canvas, 14 x 16 in.
Private collection

I did *Danse Champêtre* to give myself a chance to paint the human body again, and not simply models posing in the studio. I'm insanely old-fashioned—I'm too old-fashioned for the last century, let alone this one. An abstract painter once accused me of subscribing to the hierarchy of subject matter. In other words, I believe that historical painting is the most important. Historical painting is figure composition. You might say *The Last Judgment* of Michelangelo is a historical painting, according to that concept. I believe that historical painting is superior to portrait painting, but portrait painting is superior to still life or landscape. Such beliefs are completely out of step. There is nothing more rebellious than to be a classicist at this time. When I paint these classical subjects, I see no reason to explain why I do it; but sometimes when I look back at them, I feel like I'm kind of strange doing it at all. I should be doing drawings of Porsches, or Hupmobiles, or astronauts on the moon— something really modern.

BANDWAGON (Four More Years) 1973
Oil on canvas, 84 x 90 in.
Private collection

Bandwagon (Four More Years) is a scene from the 1972 presidential campaign. There are some people on a flatbed truck, which is decorated with red-white-and-blue bunting, and they're neighbors of mine down here in the Village, on the west side of Manhattan. All these people are apparently jubilant at the prospect of four more years of Nixon, and they're making the traditional Italian gestures of contempt at me and anyone else who might have a different notion: the finger, the hand on the elbow, etc.—I tried to get them all in.

above left:

OH MOON OF ALABAMA 1972
Oil on canvas, 40 x 35 in.
Private collection

It's an all-girl band, some of them rather old, in abbreviated costumes and black stockings—part *Threepenny Opera* and part Mae West. There is a Brecht/Weil song, "Moon of Alabama." And I had seen a rerun of a Mae West movie—*She Done Him Wrong*, I think, with Cary Grant—in which there's a funny scene in a saloon. She's singing, and all she does is smile up at the moon and wink, and the men go wild. She never even bares a shoulder, but just sort of insinuates, and they go crazy.

ROARING TWENTIES 1975
Oil on canvas, 46 x 36 in.
Private collection

I painted *Roaring Twenties* when I was commissioned to do a painting about the 1920s for the national bicentennial celebration in 1976, to be reproduced as a poster. The central figure is doing the Charleston, and most of the other women have their cloche hats pulled down. In a sense it's an exercise, and it may be an essay in cuteness, but I was attracted by the subject—which is the only real motivation for me.

JOCASTA (The Infancy of an Art Critic) 1974
Oil on canvas, 21 x 24 in.
Private collection

VOLPONE AT SAN MARCO 1977
Oil on canvas, 40 x 35 in.
Collection Thyssen-Bornemisza, Lugano, Switzerland

MOSCA AND VOLPONE 1975
Oil on canvas, 14 x 16 in.
Private collection

MATRON OF THE ARTS 1978
Oil on canvas, 16 x 14 in.
Private collection

MATRONEIA 1979
Oil on canvas, 42 x 48 in.
Private collection

Commentary on
JOCASTA
MOSCA AND VOLPONE
VOLPONE AT SAN MARCO

In the mid-'70s, I did a few paintings with references to some classical literary characters. *Mosca and Volpone* are characters in the Ben Jonson play *Volpone*. It's morning, and the servant Mosca has just opened the curtains to let the light in. One of them is holding up a golden coin and admiring it, saying "How much more beautiful in the sun this is!" The play takes place in Venice, and I took advantage of the fact when I did *Volpone at San Marco*. It gave me an opportunity to paint the facade of San Marco. Here, Volpone is in the piazza San Marco with a dwarf gondolier and a wench who is wearing a tricorn on top of a powdered wig and showing a lot of bosom. The Jonson play gave me a wonderful way to paint things that interested me and to deal with the themes of avarice and lust.

Another painting with a literary source was a picture of a mother and child, which I called *Jocasta (The Infancy of an Art Critic)*. Her little boy is, of course, Oedipus. She is a still attractive but slightly haggard woman, and her baby is wearing a tuxedo. I had read a story in the newspapers about a woman who made a tiny tuxedo for her baby boy and took him to parties as her escort, and I imagined it had to be the beginning of the making of an art critic.

Commentary on
MATRON OF THE ARTS
MATRONEIA

Matron of the Arts shows another aspect of the art world I'm not mad for. The woman is a society lady at a party, sitting on the carpet in her stocking feet next to a troubadour, who is playing a lute and serenading her. She is a social counterpart to a Master of Arts— one of those people who performs an auxiliary function in the art world. She's a matron of the arts because she acts as a "handmaiden" to artists.

Matroneia is a large party scene, with the denizens of the art world and their various camp followers and hangers-on indulging in activities of, shall we say, a less than spiritual nature. I don't show them taking cocaine or smoking pot. I'm fairly innocent. But it goes on. One see pictures, and there are books. And the men are all the sort of men like *L'Indifférent*, who really has no earthly interest in these women.

Commentary on
ETHNIKON
PANETHNIKON (ill. on pp. 122–23)

ETHNIKON 1977
Oil on canvas, 42 x 48 in.
Private collection

Ethnikon is about the different races of man. I based it on the United Nations, an organization for which I have no great enthusiasm anymore. It showed figures like Idi Amin and Yassir Arafat, and other wonderful guys like that. It was a warm-up for *Panethnikon*, a hugh diptych showing all the people of the world, which I began in the fall of 1977. When I started this, I went to the U.N. and sat around in the Security Council. I bought some postcards and cut out some pictures from the newspapers. I found a picture of Brezhnev, and I found one of our friend from Uganda. I have my own drawing of Ibn Saud but all the other characters are invented. The three fair, pale people represent what they call the first world. The somnolent man, I think of as the late Warren Austin, who was the American Ambassador to the U.N. I will always cherish him because he said on the occasion of the first struggle in Palestine: "Let us hope that this will be solved in the true Christian spirit." At least one editorial pointed out to him that these hostilities were being carried out by Arabs and Jews only, and if it were done in the true Christian spirit, it might never stop. Well, it hasn't stopped yet.

above:
Study for SOVIET VISITATION IN JERUSALEM NO. 7 1974
Mixed media, 13½ x 17 in.
Private collection

below:
Study for SOVIET VISITATION IN JERUSALEM NO. 7 1974
Gouache and pencil, 11 x 15 in.
Jules & Connie Kay

Commentary on
VISIT FROM THE SECOND WORLD
PATRIARCH OF MOSCOW ON A VISIT TO JERUSALEM

I took my wife with me when I made my second trip to
Israel, so that she could see how wonderful Jerusalem was.
Jerusalem is a jewel of a city, venerable and infinitely
stratified with past cultures, crusades, invasions. Its
crenellated walls hold endless varieties of churches,
fortresses, and mosques, thrusting up spires and towers,
domes and minarets. The Dôme of the Rock glitters and
Jerusalem's stones are golden. As we entered the bat-
tlemented gates of the old city we heard the ringing of
great bronze church bells and, drawing nearer, the thud-
ding of great iron-tipped staves on the ancient paving. It
is Pimen, the holy Metropolitan of Moscow, who had come
to take title to church properties of the surviving White
Russians in the Holy Land.

For months after my return home I was haunted by the
beauty of Jerusalem and both oppressed and intrigued by
the Russian pageant I had witnessed. It called for a large
subject painting. I began *Visit from the Second World*,
which you might say is a rehearsal for *Patriarch of Moscow
on a Visit to Jerusalem*—more improvised, more free-form
in the handling, and not nearly as large. *Patriarch* is an
enormous canvas—7 feet by 8 feet—so I worked out a lot
of the problems in the first painting. On that big a scale,
I really had to know what I was doing.

For personal reasons, I felt unable to paint Jerusalem
as it now looked to me since the unification of East and
West Jerusalem after the Six-Day War in 1967. I couldn't
set foot in East Jerusalem the first time I was there, when
it was under Arab control, and I felt intuitively that I must
show that tiny corner that I was able to see from my window at the King David Hotel a dozen years before. At the
right, I painted a group of men in Ottoman regalia with
the staves effecting a clearance through the crowds for a
mass of chanting black-robed Russian priests bearing
ikons and crosses of brass. They descend through an
archway and down steps unseen at left, among them an
ancient deacon and an acolyte swinging a censer. The
priests surround a great plump bearded patriarchal figure
clad in white with miter, crozier, and mirrored motor-
cycle goggles. In the background of the larger painting,

I added some architectural landmarks that had been visible from my window: the Church of the Nativity, a Neo-Romanesque structure with a bell tower built by the Germans early in this century. Next to it, I decided to put the Montefiore Dutch windmill given to the Jewish settlers by Sir Moses Montefiore; and since this is hardly an image of Jerusalem, I lettered the name "Jerusalem" in Hebrew. It is a scene fraught with overtones, Byzantine and enigmatic, set most strangely and disparately in Jerusalem.

One of my problems in *Patriarch of Moscow* was to show that the great white priest was a Soviet emissary. After putting in and deleting red stars and hammers and sickles, it seemed to me that a good answer was to have Brezhnev and Gromyko hiding among the priests. Since I distrusted their recognizability, I decided to print their names above them. Since I wanted clarity but not obviousness, I printed them in Russian.

I tried to do all this as though the Renaissance were imminent.

VISIT FROM THE SECOND WORLD 1974
Oil on canvas, 47 x 55¾ in.
Reynolda House, Winston-Salem, N.C.

PATRIARCH OF MOSCOW ON A VISIT TO JERUSALEM 1975
Oil on canvas, 84 x 96 in.
Collection Thyssen-Bornemisza, Lugano, Switzerland

PANETHNIKON 1978
Oil on canvas, diptych, each panel 62¼ x 72 in.
Private collection

▲
RABBI FROM PRAGUE 1974
Oil on canvas, 16¾ x 13⅞ in.
Private collection

SACRIFICE OF ISAAC 1974
Oil on canvas, 40 x 35 in.
Private collection

◄ **SHAMMAI** 1976
Oil on masonite, 19½ x 16 in.
Midtown Galleries, New York

By the time I did these particular Biblical scenes, I'd been to Israel twice and had changed my ideas about my relationship to the whole subject. I had begun to think that in the time that's left to me, there's still room to develop some kind of iconography about my Jewish identity. Of course it is also still a source of subject matter that enables me to do what I want, to roam over all the ways of painting of the past and be quite indifferent to what's going on today—or as indifferent as it's possible to be. It's been pointed out that even art forgers with the worst intentions in the world always give some indications of the time they're actually painting in.

In the *Rabbi from Prague*, I combined a traditional portrait with an architectural vignette of old Prague through the window behind the rabbi. It's a view of Prague's ghetto, showing the town hall—with its two clocks, one with Roman numerals and one with Hebrew letters—and behind that the Altneuschule, which is the oldest remaining synagogue in Europe.

In *Shammai*, by the way, I painted the word "Shammai" in Hebrew in the upper right but I misspelled it, for I didn't really know Hebrew then. I spelled it with an *ayin* instead of an *aleph*.

Sacrifice of Isaac is a sort of Shakespearean tableau of Abraham with the knife at the ready, about to plunge it into the body of his son, and behind them is a ram, one of whose horns is caught in some brambles. This, and *Jacob Wrestling with the Angel*, gave me a chance to work out late Renaissance problems such as anatomical considerations and how to capture a range of human flesh tones. Once again, it's an enabling thing.

JACOB WRESTLING WITH THE ANGEL 1975
Oil on canvas, 40 x 35 in.
Midtown Galleries, New York

◄ **Final draft study for SHAMMAI** 1976
Charcoal on tracing paper, 21 x 17 in.
Midtown Galleries, New York

OLD MORTALITY 1979
Oil on canvas, 63 x 72 in.
The Oklahoma Art Center, Oklahoma City

One day Ruth and I took the train out to the Hamptons, and as we passed a cemetery a row of policeman wearing white gloves fired their rifles into the air. It was the funeral of a high-ranking official, and Ruth suggested that I do a sort of companion piece to *Gangster Funeral* (which had also been her idea) and give equal time to the funeral of a respectable citizen. *Old Mortality* shows the funeral of a high-ranking policeman, with a crowd of relatives and dignitaries at the cemetery and a row of policemen firing their rifles, just like the scene I saw from the train. During this period, I was solving most of the problems of each piece in preliminary drawings, before I began the actual painting, and then only a minimal amount of work was necessary to bring it off. *Old Mortality* is basically a transparent golden tonality with a brown drawing in it, and just touches of color—very rubato, as they say. It is also suffused with a premonitory feeling, since Ruth was very ill at the time.

I'd like to point out that whereas my generation had come out of the Depression and the industrial struggles of the '30s, and knew that cops were hostile to anyone who didn't have an economic stake in the established order, most young people in the '60s and '70s had been taught in school that the cop was their friend and that they could trust him. And they trusted him until they began demonstrating and he laid a nightstick on them, and then they went into shock. Now, I'm a respectable, well-to-do citizen of a certain age, and the cops are all younger than I am and call

me "Sir." Despite this newfound harmony with the forces of law and order, however, because of my early experiences I still feel deep down like an adversary of the establishment.

AT THE PRECINCT 1979
Oil on canvas, 21 x 24 in.
The West Collection, West Publishing Co.
1981 Purchase Award, Copyright 1981

The subject of *At the Precinct* came out of a not very well-known painting by Degas of an Algerian who's been placed under arrest, which Degas probably modeled after a news photograph. I always like the format that Degas came up with there, and I decided to try my own hand at it. I painted the arrested man's shoulder in gold highlights, and I considered calling it *The Man with the Golden Arm*, but I was prevailed upon to use the less colorful title.

I was once taken into police custody myself. There had been a murder in a hotel lobby in Boston, and they were looking for a young man with his coat collar turned up and his hat turned down. I was picked up at a late-night cafeteria, where I was hanging around with some other seedy intellectual types. The police took me down to the station and interrogated me until the small hours of the morning, having assumed that I was a stray. When they found out that I had four brothers and three sisters and that I lived with my family in Boston, they let me go.

The '80s

The most important thing about the '80s is that my wife died—on April 2, 1982. It's something I'll never really recover from. Looking back at my behavior around that time, I realize that I wasn't operating with a full deck. After a while I got hold of myself and began to function, but it was a hell of a setback.

Although I'm not a whit more religious than I ever was—which is to say, damn little—I've been approaching my own Hebraism in a different way. I've been studying Hebrew for the last two years, quite intensively. It's very difficult, but I've found that it's worth it for its own sake. When I started it I contended, just as a matter of honesty, that I felt I should know Hebrew because people *think* I do, having seen the paintings in which I used Hebrew lettering. If I'm supposed to be such a rabbi, why don't I know the language? By now, I've also been to Israel five times, most recently in 1985, to teach painting at the University of Haifa summer school, and a year later to visit the friends I'd made in Israel over the years. I'm still fascinated with its ancient history—I've kept up my subscription to *Biblical Archaeology* and I'm always reading about digs—but I discovered on my last trip that the experience of going through the synagogues of Jerusalem gave me more of a charge than visiting the ancient relics and ruins. I've come to realize that I'm not only the last surviving Social Realist, but the first American-born artist who's painted Judaic themes; there are other American artists who have done so—such as Hyman Bloom and David Aronson—but they were born in Europe.

I'm not a sociologist, but I have a feeling that what we are now is what we're always going to be. After World War II, all we needed was more material goods and more high-tech, and we're getting everything we want. Maybe we shouldn't have it, but that's what we want. I think that the upheaval in the '60s might have been a kind of brave defiance, although in its own way it was venal. Because of conscription, basically, young people were very feisty and very militant. These kids only knew that they didn't want to be involved in whatever our generation did. At first, they were laid-back and indifferent, but they got very politicized when they thought that the young men would be drafted, and they became very active. I think that might have been only a hiatus in the drive to hedonism—that they were being interrupted on the way to the ranch house in the exurb or its equivalent. I really believe that the '80s have been much more conformist than the '50s ever were.

In the arts, too, conformity has become increasingly widespread. I think that in a sense there's been a moral deterioration since the market for American art developed in the '60s. During much of my life, American paintings weren't worth much at all. Unlike the *peintres maudits* in Paris, an artist couldn't even get a meal or a bottle of wine for a painting when I was starting out. But that all changed, and suddenly it was possible, after the long dry season for American art, to sell a painting by an American artist. There were dealers and galleries selling American art, and all sorts of people jumped in as investment counselors. They began to buy things for great corporations, for the great skyscrapers going up all over. And the whole new art business provided a tremendous largesse for all sorts of hangers-on and camp followers. Before that, artists tended to have rather strong political and social attitudes, and tended to be sermonizers and moralists. Now it's just a question of what's going to "go." What are they painting now, what are they showing at the Whitney, what's "on." I think there should never be anything

MOSES ON SINAI 1984
Oil on wood, 9¾ x 7⅝ in.
Susanna Levine Fisher

"on." I'm rather irascible about the whole thing, I admit, but, in my book, art should never be a matter of fashion. It became that with Louis XIV, and during that period the art was dreadful. Nowadays, the powers-that-be in the art business have been getting more and more concentrated, with the whole thing run by a few very influential people, and vast quantities of capital invested—especially by some of the newer players, like the Saatchis. I try to have nothing to do with it, and to avoid the whole scene altogether. As soon as I could get enough of a price for a painting—which was about thirty years ago—I quit teaching; and in the '80s, as soon as I had my Social Security and a few little packages I had set aside for myself, I was able to quit the art business and the gallery I'd been with for 15 years, to my intense delight. I simply wanted to paint without any of this superstructure around, and that's what I'm doing.

A certain critic of the opposition once said of me that I had everything it took to be an artist of great importance. Only one thing was lacking: I had not seen the burning bush—the burning bush that the Abstract Expressionists had presumably seen through the bottoms of their beer glasses in the Cedar Tavern. Who are these people, anyway? I come of people who do not even acknowledge Jesus Christ. Why am I supposed to acknowledge Abstract Expressionism? (The Italian artist Renato Guttoso once told me that there were two subjects you could not discuss in front of Picasso: death and Abstract Expressionism.) I am sick of the great artistic revelations that go from one decade to another. I go my own way. Mine is an individual expression.

I feel that in this art business, I am an outsider. Most artists like to think of themselves as rugged individualists—as independent characters. But they are usually pussycats. I think I really am an outsider. I am a little dog that goes the wrong way—under the hoop. I still believe that I have some mission in life to say what I think about the world. And let the avant-garde go hang. As far as I'm concerned, I want to remain the mean little man I always was.

ADAM AND EVE (Expulsion) 1981
Oil on canvas, 48 x 41½ in.
Collection of the artist

In 1981, when my wife was terminally ill, my thoughts returned to the archetypal couple, Adam and Eve. I was so frightened and worried at that time, I almost couldn't cope; but I tried to keep on working, and I ended up doing several paintings on this theme. I wanted to find out what I thought, and I suppose these are meditations on the relationship between man and woman, but without coming to any conclusions. I didn't have myself in hand, so they're also quite uneven. There are all sorts of distortions and inequalities that I didn't plan, that were completely inadvertent. Some of the phrasing, particularly in the musculature of the figures, is original for me; but I couldn't bring off a unity, which is difficult even in the best of times. I simply didn't have the control, and it took me a few years to get ahold of myself.

ADAM AND EVE (Eve Offers the Apple to Adam) ca. 1981
Oil on canvas, 48 x 42 in.
Collection of the artist

CAIN AND ABEL 1983 ▶
Oil on canvas, 48 x 42 in.
Collection of the artist

This *Cain and Abel* is a more lyrical version of the 1961 *Cain and Abel* (which is in the Vatican Museums). The earlier version is more drastic, and perhaps it's a somewhat more epic treatment of the theme; but this one has nuances and graces that the other one lacks. There, Cain is a real brute; he's brandishing a jawbone, which is his weapon, and he's holding Abel down and is about to smash him. Here, Cain has already killed Abel and is standing next to him, holding a large stone and contemplating what he has done.

I've always been interested in the mark of Cain, which the Almighty put on Cain's forehead not as a sign of Cain's guilt but to warn people not to molest him for what he had done. What's especially interesting about the story is that it's the first murder in the Old Testament, and in fact it's the first death. So Cain doesn't even realize what has happened—he's in a realm that he can't conceive of, and in that sense is innocent. When he saw his brother dead, he really didn't know what he had done. I did not realize this when I painted it the first time.

◄ CARNIVAL AT SUNSET 1984
Oil on canvas, 60 x 48 in.
The Butler Institute of American Art
Youngstown, Ohio

Orpheus in Vegas is an instance of my combining something satirical with something a little Rubensy and sensual. The idea of painting dancing girls was to make a point about beauty in the marketplace. I began with some dancing girls on a stage in Las Vegas, and I decided to add a singer. And when I thought of the title *Orpheus in Vegas*—parallel to a classical title such as *Iphigenia in Aulis*—I decided that the singer had to be Frank Sinatra. Although he's not *my* cup of tea, he's a very gifted entertainer, and he helps make the point about beauty and money.

Carnival at Sunset is an attempt to suggest that same point together with the idea of people being flimflammed that I first tried to express in *Medicine Show*.

ORPHEUS IN VEGAS 1984
Oil on canvas, 40 x 60 in.
Midtown Galleries, New York

ARMORERS 1981 ▶
Oil on canvas, 48 x 42 in.
Private collection

I was in Minnesota with a traveling exhibition of my work, and in Saint Paul I went to a businessman's breakfast where all the tablecloths were blood red. It was quite startling. So I decided that if I ever do a banquet scene again, I'll paint red tablecloths—no more of those white ones. Then I saw a photograph in the *Encyclopedia Britannica* of the Canadian Parliament, with all the flags of the different parts of Canada, and the effect was very colorful.

I started painting *Armorers*, and I put in a red tablecloth and an array of flags, and I populated the table with important-looking men, some in uniform and some in civvies. The figure in the center is something like a British field marshal, and he has a bright blue fourragère on his uniform, which is probably the keynote of the painting. In *The Arms Brokers* there are people like Kissinger, David Rockefeller, Reagan, and Brezhnev; and I added models

of armaments on the table and in the air. The largest model is the aircraft carrier on the table, and there's a fighter plane overhead, like Piero della Francesca's egg suspended over the Virgin Mary. I brought the men together with their toys. These are the arms brokers—the biggest game in town. They are the people in this world who really matter.

Study for DAVID AND SAUL 1984
Oil on panel, 10½ x 8 in.
Private collection

I considered that it was my purpose, as time went on and I was doing more extended subjects on larger canvases, to be a propagandist for the Old Testament, for my own group, you might say. Now I'm absolutely sold on the dramatic premises and the intense possibilities of this material. The idea of painting David playing before Saul was suggested to me by a miniature in the Morgan Library. I was very intrigued by the orderly holding him down. I thought, this man is having a nervous breakdown. And there's a wonderful kind of tragic neurotic background to the idea. I have David entertaining Saul, who was quite mad, and there's a burly soldier with his hands on Saul's shoulders, calming him. And King Saul is holding a javelin. He doesn't like this kid and he knows he's going to succeed him as king and he wants to kill him then and there. But something always stops him.

I identify with Saul. I would, because I'm bad. I hate being displaced by younger people, which is what was happening with Saul. And I detest the divine favor which is given to David and not to me. So I made this Saul closer to my own age than Saul's actual age at that point in the biblical narrative.

IN THE VALLEY OF KIDRON 1983
Oil on panel, 10 x 7¾ in.
Midtown Galleries, New York

NOAH RELEASING DOVE 1986
Oil on wood, 13⅞ x 16⅞ in.
Collection of the artist

The biblical scenes that I've painted in the '80s come out of my visits to Israel and my new approach to my own identity as a Jew, but they are still studies in late Renaissance painting. None of my masters are from the 20th century—but then there's nothing in the Ten Commandments that says, Thou shalt honor thy peer group.

Because of the Second Commandment, against graven images, there is a relatively sparse pictorial record of Jewish history or the Jewish imagination. I felt the desire to fill this gap. But I am only interested in the Bible's Jewish iconography—the Old Testament, not the New Testament. I am not one of the Jews who takes an enlightened, liberal attitude about Jesus. Christ on the Cross is to me a symbol of Jewish persecution and nothing more, and I refuse to celebrate it. The Vatican once approached my gallery about my doing a painting of Saint Paul, in honor of the current pope at that time, but I would not do it.

In the Valley of Kidron is a picture of a rabbi in front of the so-called tomb of Absalom, and I actually began painting it while I was in the Valley of Kidron. *Noah Releasing Dove* is the traditional scene of Noah after the Flood, from the book of Genesis, based loosely on a fresco by Paolo Uccello in the church of S. Maria Novella, Florence.

DAVID AND SAUL 1987–89
Oil on canvas, 72 x 63 in.
Collection of the artist

VINEYARDS OF TIMNAH 1984
Oil on wood panel, 7¾ x 9¾ in.
Susanna Levine Fisher

In the past, I've used Hebraica more as a way of making technical breakthroughs in my work; now, my fascination with the subject seems to have taken the lead, a tendency that has been enhanced by my studying the Old Testament in Hebrew. Increasingly, I find that the past is very rich and that the present is not, and to speculate about a possible Hebraic iconography represents a richer prospect to me than simply painting something under my nose. By temperament and by training, I'm more inclined to deal with images in my mind and to let my imagination hold sway than to deal with images from the external world in some matter-of-fact documentary fashion.

Samson and the Lion and *Vineyards of Timnah* are both something in between studies of musculature—to show off my command of anatomy—and attempts to do a real Jewish icon. Both are on the theme of Samson struggling with the lion, from the Book of Judges. After he killed the lion, Samson discovered that bees had nested in the lion's body and produced honey. The story makes an analogy between strength and sweetness, but I don't think I conveyed that idea very effectively. *Samson and the Lion* captures more of the spirit of Rubens's painting of Hercules and the lion than of the biblical story of Samson that was my ostensible subject. And *Vineyards of Timnah* is not unlike Pollaiuolo's painting of the centaur Charon carrying off Deianeira, the wife of Hercules, of which Dürer did a free copy.

SAMSON AND THE LION 1983
Oil on canvas, 24 x 21 in.
Private collection

◀ **RABBI IN WHITE** 1984–88
Oil on canvas, 9⅞ x 7¹³⁄₁₆ in.
Collection of the artist

Although I started *Rabbi in White* with the idea of painting a rabbi, by the time I finished it he had become a simple workingman in ritual garments. I had the idea of adding a little wooden synagogue, the kind you'd see in pictures of Eastern Europe in the old days.

KRONOS 1983
Oil on canvas, 24 x 21 in.
Collection of the artist

I thought that this would be a self-portrait when I'm 80. He's looking at his watch. He's Kronos, the god of time, who devours his young. which time does anyway. Well, I called it *Kronos* because I was looking for something to hang a painting on. The young that are being devoured represent all of us, I suppose. Time will do away with everyone. Although I'm kidding when I describe it as a portrait of myself in my 80s, I may ultimately look like that.

THE EYE OF THE BEHOLDER 1985
Oil on canvas, 28 x 20 in.
Collection of the artist

Commentary on
THE EYE OF THE BEHOLDER
AUCTION
DEALER
ON THE BLOCK

The Eye of the Beholder is the first of a series of paintings that I've been doing on the subject of my alienation from the art world and my frustrating relationships with dealers. The fundamental idea is art and money—beauty in the marketplace—which I first alluded to in *Orpheus in Vegas*. Here, I began painting so-called art lovers, subjecting them to my own judgment of who I think they are and what they are about. The title suggests perhaps that beauty isn't in the visage of the art lover—that the commercial protagonists of the art world may not make a very pretty picture themselves, physically or morally.

Auction presents a progression of four figures, ending in a figure with a skull-like face at the right. It's actually a rubber mask, which is a reference to the incident a few years

ON THE BLOCK (work in progress, 1989) ▶
Oil on canvas, 72 x 63 in.
Collection of the artist

DEALER 1986
Oil on canvas, 40 x 30 in.
Collection of the artist

AUCTION 1987
Oil on canvas, 30 x 35 in.
Collection of the artist

ago of a New York art dealer involved in the death of a young male model who was found wearing such a mask, apparently murdered in some sort of satanic ritual. I thought of it as a part of the art-world scene and I included it partly as a commentary on that scene and partly for local color. Wouldn't you?

Dealer is a single figure of a woman sitting at an auction with a pencil in her mouth. She may be bidding, or she may be marking down the prices that the artworks are fetching. She's also sitting very carelessly and showing some leg.

In *On the Block*, the largest of the series, which is still in progress, I've painted a group of these people at an auction. All of them are potential bidders, some of whom have established signals to the auctioneer. One figure has his finger up his nose, which is presumably a bid; another has his thumbs in his ears and is about to twiddle his fingers. The point is that we don't know if they're bidding or not—only the auctioneer knows. It looks a bit like an eccentric ballet. Most of the figures are completely invented, but I've included my three consecutive dealers over the fifty years that I've been showing in New York, with an expression of dislike for each one of them.

SOURCE NOTES for "Jack Levine on Jack Levine"

EDITOR'S NOTE: The text for "Jack Levine on Jack Levine" (pp.18–139) has been compiled from a variety of sources, the principal source being interviews that I conducted with him in fall 1988 and winter 1989 at his home in New York City. I edited the transcribed interviews, and then together we made revisions and adjustments in the final text. Other sources include his own writings over the years (artist's statements, catalogue essays), published interviews, and the transcript of on-camera interviews from a recent documentary film. In some instances where he has written or spoken of the same subject on different occasions, I have combined and edited his accounts into a single commentary. In the interest of clarity and accuracy, and in accord with the artist's current wishes, some small changes and corrections have been made in previously published material. Throughout, the text of the edited commentaries was reviewed by the artist and appears in the final form that he approved. All the titles of his paintings are given in this book are the definitive choice of the artist; all dates are to the best of his recollection, supported by the historical record whenever possible.

Page 18: *Jack Levine: Feast of Pure Reason*, 1985, produced and directed by David Sutherland.
Jack Levine, "My Early Boyhood," in exhib. cat., *Paintings by Jack Levine—Sculpture by David von Schlegell: Paintings and Sculpture by Americans of Our Times*, Museum of Art of Ogunquit, Maine, 1964.

19: Jack Levine, "Jack Levine Talks About the Donation of 108 of His Drawings to the Archives," *Archives of American Art Bulletin* (Detroit), vol. 2, March 1962, pp. 4–5.
Jack Levine, interviewed by Stephen Robert Frankel, fall 1988.

20: Ibid.
Jack Levine: Feast of Pure Reason (film), 1985.
Jack Levine, interviewed by Marvin Jones, *The New Common Good*, September 1986, p. 4, and October 1986, p. 6.
Jack Levine interview, *Clockwatch Review* (Hartland, Wis.), vol. 3, no. 2, 1986, p. 56.

21: Levine interview, *The New Common Good*, Oct. 1986, p. 4.
Jack Levine: Feast of Pure Reason (film), 1985.
Jack Levine, interviewed by Charles Giuliano, *Art New England*, October 1986, p. 7.

22: Ibid.
Levine interview, *The New Common Good*, Sept. 1986, p. 7.
Jack Levine: Feast of Pure Reason (film), 1985.

23: Levine, interviewed by S. R. Frankel, winter 1989.

25: Ibid., fall 1988.

26: Jack Levine, October 13, 1939, reprinted in *Art for the Millions: Essays from the 1930s by Artists and Administrators of the WPA Federal Art Project*, ed. Francis V. O'Connor (Boston: New York Graphic Society, 1973).

29: *Jack Levine: Feast of Pure Reason* (film), 1985.
Levine, interviewed by S. R. Frankel, fall 1988.

30: Ibid.
Kenneth W. Prescott, "Jack Levine: Social Commentator," in *Jack Levine*, exhib. cat. (New York: The Jewish Museum, 1978), p. 13.

31: Frederick S. Wight, "A Jack Levine Profile," *Art Digest*, vol. 26, September 15, 1952, p. 10.

32: *Jack Levine: Feast of Pure Reason* (film), 1985.
Levine, interviewed by S. R. Frankel, fall 1988.
Prescott, "Jack Levine," 1978, p. 13.

33: Levine, interviewed by S. R. Frankel, winter 1989.

34: Ibid., fall 1988.
Levine interview, *The New Common Good*, Oct. 1986, p. 6.
Levine interview, *Art New England*, Oct. 1986, pp. 7–8.

35: Levine, interviewed by S. R. Frankel, fall 1988.

36: Ibid.

37–38: Ibid.

38: Ibid.

40: Ibid., winter 1989.

41: *Jack Levine: Feast of Pure Reason* (film), 1985.
Levine, interviewed by S. R. Frankel, winter 1989.
Time Magazine, May 20, 1946, p. 64.
New York Herald Tribune, July 2, 1959.

42: Levine, interviewed by S. R. Frankel, fall 1988.

43–44: Ibid.
Jack Levine: Feast of Pure Reason (film), 1985.

44: Levine, interviewed by S. R. Frankel, winter 1989.

45: Ibid., fall 1988.

46: Levine interview, *The New Common Good*, Oct. 1986, p. 3.

47: (top) Ibid.
(bot.) Prescott, "Jack Levine," 1978, p. 22.

48: (left) Levine, interviewed by S. R. Frankel, winter 1989.
(right) Ibid., fall 1988.
Prescott, "Jack Levine," 1978, p. 17.

50: Levine, interviewed by S. R. Frankel, fall 1988.

51–52: Ibid.
Wight, "Profile," 1952, p. 10.
Prescott, "Jack Levine," 1978, p. 17.

52–53: Levine, interviewed by S. R. Frankel, fall 1988.
Prescott, "Jack Levine," 1978, p. 17.

54: Levine, interviewed by S. R. Frankel, winter 1989.

55: Ibid., fall 1988 and winter 1989.

59–62: *Jack Levine: Feast of Pure Reason* (film), 1985.
Wight, "Profile," 1952, p. 18.
Jack Levine, speech delivered at the symposium "Modern Artists on Artists of the Past," The Museum of Modern Art, April 22, 1952.

63–64: Levine, interviewed by S. R. Frankel, fall 1988 and winter 1989.

67: Ibid., fall 1988.
Prescott, "Jack Levine," 1978, p. 21.

70–71: Jack Levine, in Selden Rodman, *Conversations with Artists* (New York: Capricorn Books, 1961), pp. 195–96.
Levine, interviewed by S. R. Frankel, fall 1988 and winter 1989.

78–79: Ibid., winter 1989.

80: Ibid., fall 1988.

82: Ibid., winter 1989.

83: Ibid.

85: Ibid., fall 1988 and winter 1989.

87: (top) Ibid., winter 1989.
(bot.) Prescott, "Jack Levine," 1978, p. 22.
Levine, interviewed by S. R. Frankel, winter 1989.

88: Ibid.

89: Ibid.

91: (top) Ibid.
(bot.) *Jack Levine: Feast of Pure Reason* (film), 1985.
Prescott, "Jack Levine," 1978, p. 22.

92: Levine, interviewed by S. R. Frankel, fall 1988.

93: Ibid.
Congress Bi-Weekly (Special Issue: Dialogue in Israel) [American Jewish Congress, New York], vol. 29, no. 12, Sept. 24, 1962.
(bot.) Levine, interviewed by S. R. Frankel, winter 1989.

94: Ibid., fall 1988.

95: Ibid.

96: Ibid.

97: Ibid., fall 1988 and winter 1989.

100: Ibid., fall 1988 (except for the commentary on *Witches' Sabbath*, which Levine wrote in 1963 as an artist's statement for his gallery exhibition).

101: Ibid., fall 1988.

103: Ibid.

106: (left) Ibid., winter 1989.
(right) Ibid., fall 1988.
Prescott, "Jack Levine," 1978, p. 24.

108: (top) Levine, interviewed by S. R. Frankel, fall 1988.
Levine interview, *Clockwatch Review*, 1986, p. 55.
Levine, in Rodman, *Conversations*, 1961, p. 197.
(bot.) Levine, interviewed by S. R. Frankel, fall 1988.

109: Ibid.
Prescott, "Jack Levine," 1978, p. 23.
Levine interview, *Clockwatch Review*, 1986, p. 54.

110: Levine, interviewed by S. R. Frankel, fall 1988 and winter 1989.
Jack Levine: Feast of Pure Reason (film), 1985.
(bot.) Levine, interviewed by S. R. Frankel, fall 1988.

111: Ibid., winter 1989.
Prescott, "Jack Levine," 1978, p. 23.

112: (left) Artist's statement for ACA Galleries, ca., 1970.
(right) Levine, interviewed by S. R. Frankel, fall 1988.

113: (left) Ibid.
Prescott, "Jack Levine," 1978, p. 23.
(right) Levine, interviewed by S. R. Frankel, fall 1988.

114: (top) Ibid., winter 1989.
(bot.) Ibid., fall 1988.
Levine interview, *Clockwatch Review*, 1986, p. 52.

115: Levine, interviewed by S. R. Frankel, fall 1988.

117: Ibid.

118: *Jack Levine: Feast of Pure Reason* (film), 1985.
Prescott, "Jack Levine," 1978, p. 26.

119–20: Levine, interviewed by S. R. Frankel, fall 1988.
Prescott, "Jack Levine," 1978, p. 24.

125: Levine, interviewed by S. R. Frankel, fall 1988.

126: Ibid., winter 1989.

127: Ibid., fall 1988 and winter 1989.
Levine interview, *Clockwatch Review*, 1986, p. 62.
Jack Levine: Feast of Pure Reason (film), 1985.

128: Levine, interviewed by S. R. Frankel, winter 1989.

131: Ibid., fall 1988.

133: Ibid.
Jack Levine: Feast of Pure Reason (film), 1985.

134: (left) Levine, interviewed by S. R. Frankel, fall 1988 and winter 1989.
(right) *Jack Levine: Feast of Pure Reason* (film), 1985.

136: Levine, interviewed by S. R. Frankel, fall 1988 and winter 1989.

137–38: Ibid.

PUBLIC COLLECTIONS

Addison Gallery of American Art, Philips Academy, Andover, Mass.
The Art Institute of Chicago, Illinois
The Brooklyn Museum, New York, N.Y.
The Butler Institute of American Art, Youngstown, Ohio
Colby College Museum of Art, Waterville, Maine
DeCordova and Dana Museum and Park, Lincoln, Mass.
Des Moines Art Center, Iowa
Edwin A. Ulrich Museum of Art, Wichita State University, Kansas
The Fine Arts Museums of San Francisco, California
Fogg Art Museum, Harvard University, Cambridge, Mass.
Hirshhorn Museum and Sculpture Garden, Smithsonian Institution, Washington, D.C.
The Israel Museum, Jerusalem
The Jewish Museum, New York, N.Y.
The Jewish Theological Seminary of America, New York, N.Y.
Maier Museum of Art, Randolph-Macon Women's College, Lynchburg, Va.
Memphis Brooks Museum of Art, Tennessee
The Metropolitan Museum of Art, New York, N.Y.
Minnesota Museum of Art, St. Paul, Minn.
The Montclair Art Museum, New Jersey
Montgomery Museum of Fine Arts, Alabama
Munson-Williams-Proctor Institute of Modern Art, Utica, N.Y.
Museum of Art, University of Oklahoma, Norman
Museum of Fine Arts, Boston
The Museum of Modern Art, New York, N.Y.
The National Gallery of Art, Washington, D.C.
National Museum of American Art, Smithsonian Institution, Washington, D.C.
Neuberger Museum, State University of New York at Purchase
New Jersey State Museum, Trenton
The Oklahoma Art Center, Oklahoma City
The Pennsylvania Academy of the Fine Arts, Philadelphia
The Phillips Collection, Washington, D.C.
Portland Art Museum, Oregon
Reed College, Portland, Oregon
Reynolda House, Winston-Salem, N.C.
Rose Art Museum, Brandeis University, Waltham, Mass.
San Francisco Museum of Modern Art, California
Santa Barbara Museum of Art, California
Seattle Art Museum, Washington
Sheldon Swope Art Gallery, Terre Haute, Ind.
Spencer Museum of Art, University of Kansas, Lawrence
Thyssen-Bornemisza Collection, Lugano, Switzerland
University of Arizona Museum of Art, Tucson
University of Iowa Museum of Art, Iowa City
University of Nebraska Art Galleries, Lincoln
Vatican Museums, Rome
Walker Art Center, Minnesota
Whitney Museum of American Art, New York, N.Y.
The Wichita Art Museum, Kansas
William Benton Museum of Art, University of Connecticut, Storrs
Williams College Museum of Art, Williamstown, Mass.

SELECTED SOLO EXHIBITIONS

1939
The Downtown Gallery, New York, N.Y., *Jack Levine.*
1948
The Downtown Gallery, *Jack Levine: Exhibition of New Paintings.*
1950
Boris Mirski Gallery, Boston, Mass., *Jack Levine.*
1952–55
Institute of Contemporary Art, Boston, Mass., *Jack Levine Retrospective Exhibition.* Traveled to: The Currier Gallery of Art, Manchester, N.H., 1952; Colorado Springs Fine Arts Center, Colorado, 1953; Akron Art Institute, Ohio, 1953; The Phillips Collection, Washington, D.C., 1953; Whitney Museum of American Art, New York, 1955.
1953
The Alan Gallery, New York, N.Y.
1956
Colby College, Waterville, Maine, *Jack Levine.*
1960
Randolph-Macon Women's College, Lynchburg, Va., *49th Annual Exhibition: Paintings by Jack Levine.*
Instituto Nacional de Bellas Artes, Mexico City, *Jack Levine.*
1968
Galeria Coliri, San Juan, Puerto Rico, *Jack Levine: Dreigroschenfilm.*
DeCordova Museum, Lincoln, Mass. *Jack Levine: Retrospective Exhibition.*
Galleria d'Arte il Gabbiano, Rome, *Jack Levine: Opera Graphica.*
1972
Kennedy Galleries, New York, N.Y., *Jack Levine: Recent Paintings.*
1978–80
The Jewish Museum, New York, N.Y., *Jack Levine: Retrospective Exhibition—Paintings, Drawings, Graphics.* Traveled to: Norton Gallery and School of Art, West Palm Beach, Fla., 1979; Brooks Memorial Art Gallery, Memphis, Tenn., 1979; Montgomery Museum of Fine Arts, Ala., 1979; Portland Art Museum, Ore., 1979; Minnesota Museum of Art, St. Paul, Minn., 1979–80.

SELECTED GROUP EXHIBITIONS

1936
The Museum of Modern Art, New York, N.Y., *New Horizons in American Art.*
1937
The Downtown Gallery, New York, N.Y., *Twelve Young American Painters.*
Whitney Museum of American Art, New York, N.Y., *Annual Exhibition of Contemporary American Painting.* Also represented in other Whitney annual exhibitions: 1938, 1940, 1941, 1942, 1945, 1948, 1949, 1950, 1951, 1952, 1953, 1955, 1956, 1957, 1959, 1960, 1961, 1963, 1965, 1967.
1938
Three Centuries of American Art, organized by the Museum of Modern Art, exhibited at the Musée du Jeu de Paume, Paris.
Carnegie Institute, Pittsburgh, Pa., *International Exhibition of Paintings.* Also represented in other Carnegie Institute annual exhibitions: 1939, 1945, 1946, 1947, 1948, 1949, 1950, 1955.
1939
New York World's Fair, New York, N.Y., *American Art Today.*
The Museum of Modern Art, *Tenth Anniversary Exhibition: Art in Our Time.*
1940
Pennsylvania Academy of the Fine Arts, Philadelphia, Pa., *135th Exhibition of Painting and Sculpture.* Also represented in other Pennsylvania Academy annual exhibitions: 1941, 1942, 1943, 1944, 1948, 1949, 1950, 1951, 1952, 1954, 1956, 1957, 1958, 1962, 1964, 1966, 1967, 1968.

The Museum of Modern Art, in collaboration with the WPA Federal Art Program, *Four American Travelling Exhibitions.*
Carnegie Institute, Pittsburgh, Pa., *Survey of American Painting.*
1940–41
The Museum of Modern Art, *Thirty-five Under Thirty-five.* Traveled to eight other U.S. institutions.
1942
The Museum of Modern Art, *Americans 1942, 18 Artists from 9 States.* Traveled to Institute of Contemporary Art, Boston, Mass.
City Art Museum, St. Louis, Mo., *Thirty-sixth Annual American Exhibition: Trends in American Painting of Today.*
The Metropolitan Museum of Art, New York, N.Y., *Artists for Victory: An Exhibition of Contemporary American Art.*
1943
Milwaukee Art Institute, Milwaukee, Wisc., *Masters of Contemporary American Painting.*
Corcoran Gallery of Art, Washington, D.C., *18th Biennial Exhibition of Contemporary American Oil Paintings.* Also represented in other Corcoran biennial exhibitions: 1947, 1959.
1945–48
Encyclopaedia Britannica Collection of Contemporary American Painting, organized by Encyclopaedia Britannica, Inc., Chicago, Ill.; opened at the Art Institute of Chicago, and traveled to 36 U.S. cities.
1946
National Academy of Design, New York, N.Y., *Second Annual Exhibition of Contemporary American Drawing.*
The Tate Gallery, London, *American Painting from the Eighteenth Century to the Present.*
1947
The Brooklyn Museum, Brooklyn, N.Y., *Anniversary Exhibition.*
Institute of Contemporary Art, Boston, Mass., *30 Massachusetts Painters in 1947.*
1947–48
American Industry Sponsors Art, organized by the U.S. Department of State and traveled in Europe.
1949–50
Institute of Contemporary Art, Boston, *American Painting in Our Century.* Traveled to five U.S. institutions.
University of Illinois, Urbana, *Contemporary American Painting.*
1950
The Metropolitan Museum of Art, *American Painting Today.*
1951
The Art Institute of Chicago, *60th Annual Exhibition: Paintings and Sculpture.* Also represented in the Art Institute of Chicago annual exhibitions of 1959 and 1964.
Museu de Arte Moderna de São Paulo, Brazil, *I São Paulo Bienal.*
1952
Whitney Museum of American Art, *Edith and Milton Lowenthal Collection.* Traveled to Walker Art Center, Minneapolis, Minn.
1953
Seattle Art Museum, Wash., *Contemporary American Painting and Sculpture.*
1955–56
Modern Art in the U.S.A., organized by the Museum of Modern Art. Traveled to: Musée National d'Art Moderne, Paris; Kunsthaus, Zurich; Museo del Art Moderno, Barcelona; Haus des Deutschen Kunsthandwerks, Frankfurt; The Tate Gallery, London, 1956; Gemeentemuseum, The Hague, 1956; Neue Gallerie in der Stallburg, Vienna, 1956; Kalemagdan Pavilion, Belgrade, 1956.
1956
Venice, *XXVIII Biennale di Venezia.*
1957
Solomon R. Guggenheim Museum, New York, N.Y., *First Annual Guggenheim International Award Exhibition.*
1958
Instituto Nacional de Bellas Artes, Mexico City, *I Bienal Interamericana de Pintura y Grabado.*
Pennsylvania Academy of the Fine Arts, *20th Century Painting and Sculpture from Philadelphia Private Collections.*

1958–59
Fulbright Painters, organized by the Smithsonian Institution, Washington, D.C., and traveled to 20 U.S. cities; opened at the Whitney Museum of American Art, New York.
1959
Whitney Museum of American Art, *The Museum and Its Friends: Eighteen Living American Artists Selected by the Friends of the Whitney Museum.*
American Painting and Sculpture, organized by the U.S. Department of State; opened in Moscow, U.S.S.R.
Association of Museums in Israel, Jerusalem, *18 American Artists,* sponsored by the Whitney Museum of American Art and American Federation of Arts, New York, N.Y.
1960
The Metropolitan Museum of Art, *The Nate and Frances Spingold Collection.*
1962–66
ART: USA: NOW: The Johnson Collection of Contemporary American Paintings, organized by S.C. Johnson and Son, Inc. Traveled to U.S. cities, Europe, and Japan for five years.
1963
The Beaverbrook Art Gallery, Fredericton, England, *The Dunn International: An Exhibition of Contemporary Painting.* Traveled to the Tate Gallery, London.
1963–64
National Gallery of Art, Washington, D.C., *Paintings from the Museum of Modern Art, New York.*
1964
Galleria George Lester, Rome, *Paintings, Jack Levine, The Judgment of Paris; Collages, Nathan Oliveira.*
1965
The Metropolitan Museum of Art, *Three Centuries of American Painting.*
1966
Corcoran Gallery, Washington, D.C., *Two Hundred and Fifty Years of American Art.*
1967
Vatican Museums, Rome, *American Graphics Exhibited at the Museum of Contemporary Art, Vatican Museums.*
1968
Whitney Museum of American Art, *The 1930's: Painting and Sculpture in America.*
1971
The Museum of Modern Art, *The Artist as Adversary.*
1974
The American Academy of Arts and Letters and the National Institute of Arts and Letters, New York, N.Y., *Annual Ceremonial and Exhibition of Works by Newly Elected Members.*
1975–76
The Jewish Museum, New York, N.Y., *Jewish Experience in the Art of the Twentieth Century.*
1977–78
Representations of America, co-organized by the Metropolitan Museum of Art and the Fine Arts Museums of San Francisco. Traveled in the U.S.S.R. to: Pushkin Museum, Moscow, 1977–78; Hermitage Museum, Leningrad, 1978; Palace of Art, Minsk, 1978.
1978
Montgomery Museum of Fine Arts, Montgomery, Ala., *American Art 1934–1956: Selections From the Whitney Museum of American Art.* Traveled to: Brooks Memorial Art Gallery, Memphis, Tenn.; Mississippi Museum of Art, Jackson, Miss.
1982
Oklahoma Art Center, Oklahoma City, *American Masters of the Twentieth Century.* Traveled to: Terra Museum of American Art, Evanston, Ill.

Bibliography

WRITINGS BY LEVINE (arranged chronologically)

"Jack Levine," in *Americans 1942—18 Artists from 9 States.* Ed. by Dorothy C. Miller. New York: The Museum of Modern Art, 1942. [exhib. cat.]

Statement on *String Quartet* in "Notes." *The Metropolitan Museum of Art Bulletin*, vol. 7, February 1949, p. 148.

"Form and Content." *College Art Journal*, vol. 9, Autumn 1949, pp. 57–58.

"Man Is the Center." *Reality; A Journal of Artists' Opinions* (New York), vol. 1, Spring 1953, pp. 5–6 (abridged from a speech delivered in a symposium, "Modern Artists on Artists of the Past," held at the Museum of Modern Art, Apr. 22, 1952).

"Jack Levine Talks about the Donation of 108 of His Drawings to the Archives." *Archives of American Art Bulletin*, vol. 2, March 1962, pp. 4–5.

"My Early Boyhood," in *Paintings by Jack Levine—Sculpture by David von Schlegell: Paintings and Sculpture by Americans of Our Times.* Museum of Art of Ogunquit, Maine, 1964. [exhib. cat.]

"In Praise of Knowledge," in *The Influence of Spiritual Inspiration on American Art.* Musei Vaticani and the Smithsonian Institution. Rome: Libreria Editrice Vaticana, 1977, pp. 55–60.

"Some Technical Aspects of Easel Painting," in *WPA Art for the Millions: Essays from the 1930s by Artists and Administrators of the WPA Federal Art Project.* Ed. by Francis V. O'Connor. Boston: New York Graphic Society, Ltd., 1973, pp. 117–20.

Jack Levine/Kennedy Galleries. New York: Kennedy Galleries, 1975. [exhib. cat.]

MONOGRAPHS

Getlein, Frank. *Jack Levine.* New York: Harry N. Abrams, Inc., 1966.

Prescott, Kenneth. *Jack Levine.* New York: The Jewish Museum, 1978. [exhib. cat.]

Prescott, Kenneth, and Prescott, Emma-Stina. *The Complete Graphic Work of Jack Levine.* New York: Dover Press, 1986.

SELECTED BOOKS

Art in Progress. New York: The Museum of Modern Art, 1944.

Barr, Alfred H., Jr., ed. *Masters of Modern Art.* New York: The Museum of Modern Art, 1955, pp. 158, 228.

Baur, John I. H. *Revolution and Tradition in Modern American Art.* Cambridge, Mass.: Harvard University Press, 1951, pp. 20, 44, 133, 143.

Geldzahler, Henry. *American Painting in the Twentieth Century.* Greenwich, Conn.: New York Graphic Society, 1965, pp. 111–14, 219.

Genauer, Emily. *Best of Art.* Garden City, N.Y.: Doubleday, 1948, pp. 5–6.

Green, Samuel. *American Art.* New York: Ronald Press Co., 1966, pp. 566, 569–71.

Miller, Dorothy. *New Horizons in American Art.* New York: The Museum of Modern Art, 1936.

_____, ed. *Americans 1942.* New York: The Museum of Modern Art, 1942, pp. 86–92.

Rodman, Selden. *Conversations with Artists.* New York: Devin-Adar, 1957. Reprinted by Chronicle Books, 1961, pp. 194–97.

Shenker, Israel. *Coat of Many Colors.* Garden City, N.Y.: Doubleday & Company, Inc., 1985, pp. 263–66.

Soby, James Thrall. *Contemporary Painters.* New York: Museum of Modern Art, 1948, pp. 69–70.

_____. "Gangster's Funeral," in *Modern Art and the New Past.* Norman, Okla.: University of Oklahoma Press, 1957, pp. 187–92.

Spencer, Charles. "Jack Levine: Protest Painter," in *The Jew: Quest 2.* London: Cornmarket Press Ltd., 1967, pp. 24–32.

Teachers and Kings: Six Paintings by Jack Levine. Intro. by Paul J. Sachs. Greenwich, Conn.: New York Graphic Society, 1959.

SELECTED PERIODICALS

(arranged chronologically)

[* indicates that article is an exhibition review]

Art Digest, vol. 11, Oct. 1, 1936, cover.

*Davidson, Martha. "The Government as a Patron of Art." *Art News*, vol. 35, Oct. 10, 1936, pp. 11–12.

*Mumford, Lewis. "The Art Galleries." *New Yorker*, vol. 10, Oct. 10, 1936.

*"Twelve." *Time*, vol. 30, Oct. 18, 1937.

*D[avidson], M[artha]. "Levine: Epic Painting in a First One-man Showing." *Art News*, vol. 37, Jan. 1939, p. 12.

*Bird, Paul. "The Fortnight in New York." *Art Digest*, vol. 13, Feb. 1, 1939, pp. 18–19.

Parnassus, vol. 13, February 1941, p. 92.

*"Downtown Group." *Art Digest*, vol. 15, June 1, 1941, p. 24.

Crowninshield, Frank. "Six American discoveries—A great museum goes to the artists." *Vogue*, vol. 99, May 15, 1942.

*"No More K.P." *Art Digest*, vol. 17, Jan. 1, 1943, p. 12.

*"Britannica Collection Fulfills Promise." *Art Digest*, vol. 19, Sept. 15, 1945, p. 5f.

*Breuning, Margaret. "This Is Their Best." *Art Digest*, vol. 20, Nov. 15, 1945, p. 31.

"Angry Artist." *Time*, vol. 47, May 20, 1946, p. 64.

*"The Found and the Lost." *Newsweek*, vol. 27, May 20, 1946.

*"The American Taste." *Time*, vol. 47, June 24, 1946.

*"The Big Show." *Time*, vol. 48, Oct. 21, 1946.

*"Carnegie Goes Abstract." *Newsweek*, vol. 28, Oct. 21, 1946, p. 106.

Frankfurter, Alfred M. "American Art Abroad." *Art News*, vol. 45, October 1946, p. 26.

*Louchheim, Aline B. "One More Carnegie." *Art News*, vol. 45, November 1946, p. 40.

*Thwaites, John Anthony. "London Letter; The Tate Show: Misrepresenting American Art." *Magazine of Art*, vol. 39, December 1946, pp. 382–83.

*Boswell, Peyton. "Review of the Year." *Art Digest*, vol. 21, Jan. 1, 1947, p. 18f.

"Americans Abroad." *Magazine of Art*, vol. 40, January 1947, pp. 21–25.

*"Corcoran Biennial Opens in Washington—Menkes Places First." *Art Digest*, vol. 21, Apr. 1, 1947, p. 12f.

"*Welcome Home* Acquired by the Museum." *Brooklyn Institute of Arts and Sciences Bulletin*, vol. 8, Mar. 1947, p. 2.

Summers, Marion. "From the Sketchbook of Jack Levine." *Mainstream* (New York), vol. 1, Spring 1947, pp. 213–16.

McCausland, Elizabeth. "The Caustic Art of Jack Levine." *'47 Magazine of the Year* (New York), vol. 1, September 1947.

*Dame, Lawrence. "Regarding Boston." *Art Digest*, vol. 22, Jan. 1, 1948, p. 14f.

*Breuning, Margaret. "Five of the Best." *Art Digest*, vol. 22, Feb. 1, 1948, p. 10.

*"Reviews and Previews: Five Americans." *Art News*, vol. 46, February 1948, p. 58.

"The School of Boston." *Newsweek*, vol. 31, May 5, 1948.

*Exhibition, Downtown Gallery." *Pictures on Exhibit*, vol. 10, May 1948, pp. 18–19ff.

*"Spotlight on: Levine, Berman, Arnest, Lam." *Art News*, vol. 47, May 1948, p. 36f.

*Dame, Lawrence. "Boston Institute Surveys American Painting." *Art Digest*, vol. 23, Feb. 1, 1949, p. 12f.

*"Handful of Fire." *Time*, vol. 55, Dec. 26, 1949.

"The Image of Man: The Artist Has Shattered It, but He Cannot Forget It." *Life*, vol. 27, Jan. 23, 1950.

*"City Boy." *Time*, vol. 55, Jan. 30, 1950, p. 51.

"Itinerant General: Levine's *Welcome Home*." *Brooklyn Institute of Arts and Sciences Bulletin*, vol. 12, Fall 1950, p. 4.

Meyers, Bernard. "Jack Levine, One of the Most Versatile Painters in the World Today." *American Artist*, vol. 15, Summer 1951, pp. 36–41.

*"Crises and Dilemma: Retrospective Show at Boston's Institute of Contemporary Art." *Time*, vol. 60, Sept. 8, 1952, pp. 82–83.

*Wight, Frederick S. "A Jack Levine Profile." *Art Digest*, vol. 26, Sept. 15, 1952, pp. 10–11f.

*"Breakthroughs." *Time*, vol. 62, Nov. 16, 1953, p. 84.

Soby, James Thrall. "Gangster's Funeral." *Saturday Review* (Washington, D.C.), vol. 36, Dec. 5, 1953, pp. 57–58.

*"Bucking the Trend." *Time*, vol. 64, Oct. 18, 1954.

*Coates, Robert M. "The Art Galleries: Retrospective Works of Hyman Bloom and Jack Levine at the Whitney." *New Yorker*, vol. 31, Mar. 12, 1955, pp. 100–102.

*"Fortnight in Review: Hyman Bloom and Jack Levine." *Art Review*, vol. 29, no. 12, Mar. 15, 1955, p. 22

"The Angry Art of the Thirties." *Fortune*, vol. 51, March 1955.

*"Major Work by an American Artist Shown with Preliminary Drawings." *The Art Institute of Chicago Quarterly*, vol. 49, Apr. 1, 1955, p. 23ff.

*Schack, William. "Genesis and Kings." *The Reconstructionist* (New York), vol. 21, June 24, 1955.

*Kramer, Hilton. "Bloom and Levine: The Hazards of Modern Painting." *Commentary*, vol. 19, June 1955, pp. 583–87.

*"Splendid Handful." *Time*, vol. 66, Aug. 8, 1955, p. 56.

Johnson, Una E. "Contemporary American Drawings." *Perspectives USA*, no. 13, Oct. 1955, p. 94.

"The Trial." *University of Chicago Magazine*, vol. 48, March 1956.

*"Poison in the Sky." *Time*, vol. 68, Sept. 24, 1956, p. 74.

"*String Quartet* by Jack Levine." *Etude* (Philadelphia), vol. 74 October 1956.

*Coates, Robert M. "Art Galleries: Male and Female." *New Yorker*, vol. 33, May 18, 1957, pp. 129–30.

Getlein, Frank. "Jack Levine: The Degrees of Corruption." *The New Republic*, Oct. 6, 1958, p. 20.

Grossman, Emery. "Jack Levine: Young Dean of American Artists." *Temple Israel Light* (Great Neck, N.Y.), vol. 5, January 1959.

*"The Corcoran's Century." *Time*, vol. 73, Feb. 2, 1959, pp. 50–51.

Werner, Alfred. "The Peopled World of Jack Levine." *The Painter and Sculptor* (London), vol. 2, Summer 1959, pp. 24–29.

Werner, Alfred. "Jack Levine's Feast of Colour." *Jewish Affairs* (Johannesburg), October 1959, pp. 13–15.

*"New Work at The Alan Gallery." *Apollo* (London), vol. 70, October 1959, p. 106.

"U.S. Art to Russia; the State Department Changes Policy." *Art News*, November 1959, p. 301.

*"Easier Levine." *Time*, vol. 75, Jan. 11, 1960, p. 56.

Rivas, Guillermo. "Paintings in the Second Biennial." *Mexican Life* (Mexico City), October 1960.

Genauer, Emily. "On the Defensive." *Art Digest*, vol. 26, Oct. 1, 1961, p. 34.

"Precocious Pencil." *Time*, vol. 79, Feb. 9, 1962, p. 56.

*Getlein, Frank. "The Whitney: What's New?" *The New Republic*, vol. 146, Feb. 12, 1962, pp. 30–31.

Getlein, Frank. "Art Against the Grain." *Horizons*, vol. 4, July 1962, p. 16.

"Dialogue in Israel." *Congress Bi-Weekly (Special Issue)* (American Jewish Congress, New York), vol. 29, no. 12, Sept. 24, 1962.

*"In the Galleries: Jack Levine, Hyman Bloom." *Arts*, vol. 37, November 1962, p. 42.

Getlein, Frank. "Printmaking and the Painter." *The New Republic*, vol. 149, Oct. 5, 1963, pp. 31–33.

*Oliveira, Nathan. "Alla galleria di Roma, mostra di Levine e Oliveira/Levine espone una serie di opere sul 'Giudizio di Paride.'" *Arte Oggi* (Rome), May 20, 1964.

Werner, Alfred. "The Art of Jack Levine." *The Chicago Jewish Forum*, vol. 23, Winter 1964–65.

McCoy, Garnett. "The Artist Speaks: Part V." *Art in America*, vol. 53, August–September 1965, pp. 88–107.

Werner, Alfred. "On Jack Levine, Upon the Occasion of His Appearance at the Herzl Institute." *Herzl Institute Bulletin* (New York), vol. 2, Oct. 24, 1965.

*"In the Galleries: Jack Levine." *Arts*, vol. 40, June 1966, p. 52.

Kay, Jane. "Portrait of the Artist—Jack Levine, Paintings and Prints at DeCordova Museum." *Boston Arts*, March 1968, pp. 19–21.

Carriere, Raffaele. "Jack Levine: Un americano affamato di immagini." *Epoca*, vol. 19, June 1968, pp. 139–41.

"The Democrats After Chicago." *Time*, vol. 92, Sept. 6, 1968.

Haverstock, Mary Sayre. "An American Bestiary." *Art in America*, vol. 58, July–August 1970. pp. 38–71.

Michener, James. "The Social Critic and Somber Witness on an Enchanted Holiday." *Orientations* (Hong Kong), vol. 1, October 1970, p. 24ff.

*Hancock, Marianne. "Review: Jack Levine." *Arts*, vol. 46, Summer 1972, p. 65.

Young, Mahonri Sharp. "Jack Levine: An appreciation." *North Light* (Westport, Conn.), vol. 4, November–December 1972, pp. 10–15.

Baldwin, C. "Le Penchant des peintres américains pour le réalisme." *Connaissance des Arts*, no. 254, April 1973, p. 119.

Henry, Gerrit. "Jack Levine: 'If I were doing anything else, I'd be bored to tears.'" *Art News*, vol. 78, April 1979, pp. 46–49.

Young, Mahonri Sharp. "American Realists of the 1930s: Part V. Leaning left." *Apollo* (London), March 1981, pp. 177–79.

Halasz, Piri. "Figuration in the '40s; the Other Expressionism." *Art in America*, December 1982.

Corbino, Marcia. "The Art World According to Jack Levine." *American Artist*, vol. 49, May 1985, pp. 60–65ff.

"An interview with social realist painter Jack Levine." *Clockwatch Review* (Hartland, Wisc.), vol. 3, no. 2, 1986, pp. 50–62.

SELECTED NEWSPAPER ARTICLES

(arranged chronologically)
[*indicates that article is an exhibition review]

*"The Federal Art Show." *Christian Science Monitor*, Apr. 27, 1937.

*Jewell, Edward Alden. "Lively Americans at the Whitney." *The New York Times*, Nov. 14, 1937.

*"Paintings by Whorf and Levine Chosen for Paris Exhibition." *Boston Evening Transcript*, Apr. 30, 1938.

*Genauer, Emily. "Downtown Exhibits Bitter Protests of Jack Levine." *New York World-Telegram*, Jan. 21, 1939.

*"Exhibition, The Downtown Gallery." *The New York Times*, Jan. 22, 1939.

*"Contemporary American Art Put on Display." *New York Herald Tribune*, Jan. 2, 1942.

*Adlow, Dorothy. "Artists for Victory Show Under Art Institute Auspices." *Christian Science Monitor*, June 1, 1943.

*Genauer, Emily. "Changes in Technique." *New York World-Telegram*, Dec. 1, 1945.

Brooks, Ned. "Modern Art Banned as Official Export." *New York World-Telegram*, May 19, 1947.

*Genauer, Emily. "Vital Works on View by Levine." *New York World-Telegram*, May 11, 1948.

*Genauer, Emily. "*Welcome Home* Gets Reception at Denver Show." *New York World-Telegram*, Aug. 24, 1948.

DeVree, Howard. "Purchases" [*Reception in Miami* . . . Among Recent Museum Acquisitions]. *The New York Times*, Jan. 2, 1949.

*Driscoll, Edgar J., Jr. "Levine's One-Man Show Stimulating Exhibit." *Boston Sunday Globe*, Jan. 22, 1950.

*Taylor, Robert. "A Major American Artist Emerges From the South End." *Boston Sunday Herald*, Sept. 21, 1952.

*Driscoll, Edgar J., Jr. "Levine Show Highlights New Boston Art Season." *Boston Sunday Globe*, Sept. 28, 1952.

*Werner, Alfred. "Art and Artists." *Congress Weekly* (New York), Oct. 13, 1952.

*Genauer, Emily. "Humanist with Bite." *New York Herald Tribune*, May 31, 1953.

*DeVree, Howard. "From Old Masters to American Moderns Range the Week's Exhibitions." *The New York Times*, Oct. 4, 1953.

*"Levine Work Monumental." *New York Herald Tribune*, Oct. 31, 1953.

Werner, Alfred. "Art and Artists." *Congress Weekly*, (New York), Dec. 7, 1953.

*DeVree, Howard. "Whitney Museum Opens Retrospective Shows of Work by Levine and Bloom." *The New York Times*, Feb. 24, 1955.

*Genauer, Emily. "Two Realists at the Whitney." *New York Herald Tribune*, Feb. 27, 1955.

*Driscoll, Edgar J., Jr. "Three Flights Up But Worth Climb." *Boston Sunday Globe*, Dec. 14, 1958.

Donovan, Robert J. "President Is Critical of Art for Moscow." *New York Herald Tribune*, July 2, 1959.

*Canaday, John. "Two American Painters." *The New York Times*, Jan. 3, 1960, p. 18.

*Genauer, Emily. "The Future in Art? A Critic's Answers." *New York Herald Tribune*, Jan. 3, 1960.

*Burrows, Carlyle. "Style Change Best for Guston, Status Quo Good for Levine." *New York Herald Tribune*, Jan. 3, 1960.

*Levin, Meyer, and Levin, Eli. "Painter Levine Retains Critical, Social Perspective." *Philadelphia Enquirer*, Feb. 14, 1960.

*Vargas, Carlos. "Exposicion Retrospectiva de Obras del Pintor J. Levine." *El Universal* (Mexico City), Jul. 24, 1960.

*Porcel, Gonzales. "Habla Jack Levine Acerca de la Pintura y de la Politica." *Ultimas Noticias* (Mexico City), Sept. 14, 1960.

Ronnen, Meir. "Look Back in Anger—on Canvas." *Jerusalem Post Weekly* (Israel), June 17, 1962.

*Culhane, David M. "Londoners Get a Look at 'Art: USA: Now.'" *Sun* (Baltimore), Mar. 3, 1963.

*Genauer, Emily. "Reassuring Show by Jack Levine." *New York Herald Tribune*, Apr. 14, 1963.

Getlein, Frank. "Prints in the Great Tradition." *Sunday Star* (Washington, D.C.), Aug. 11, 1963.

*Genauer, Emily. "The Whitney Annual." *New York Herald Tribune*, Dec. 15, 1963.

Canaday, John. "Art: Debutante and a Grand Old Man." *The New York Times*, Jan. 16, 1964.

*"Il Mito del Sesso visto da Levine." *L'Unità* (Milan), May 30, 1963.

*Banks, Harold. "Jack Is Quick on the Draw." *Record American* (Boston), Sept. 4, 1964.

*Genauer, Emily. "The Facts Up to Date at the Whitney Annual." *New York Herald Tribune*, Dec. 12, 1965.

*Getlein, Frank. "Impressive Panorama of American Art at Corcoran." *Sunday Star* (Washington, D.C.), Apr. 17, 1966.

Getlein, Frank. "Art: The Summertime Boom in Graphics Is Here Again." *Washington Star*, Aug. 1967.

*"Call Him 'Jack the Brush,' *Threepenny Opera* Inspires Portfolio of Prints." *Washington Post*, Nov. 30, 1967.

Werner, Alfred. "Views and Visions." *Jewish News* (Newark, N.J.), Jan. 5, 1968.

*"Pintor Levine Ofreceria Charla." *El Mundo* (San Juan, Puerto Rico), Jan. 23, 1968.

*"Jack Levine Works at DeCordova." *Jewish Advocate* (Boston), Feb. 1, 1968.

*Ruiz de la Mata, Ernesto J. "Jack Levine." *San Juan Star Magazine* (Puerto Rico), Feb. 4, 1968.

*Driscoll, Edgar J., Jr., "Jack Levine's Acid Works of Art, Alas the human touch." *Boston Globe*, Feb. 11, 1968.

*LeBrun, Caron. "At Last—A Tribute to Jack Levine." *Herald Traveler* (Boston), Mar. 17, 1968.

"Americani del dissenso." *L'Unità* (Milan), Apr. 5, 1968.

*"L'arte polemica di Jack Levine." *Paese Sera* (Rome), Apr. 5, 1968.

Berkman, Florence. "'Non-Artists Have Called the Shots,' Says Levine." *Hartford Times* (Conn.), Mar. 18, 1969.

*Wallach, Amei. "The Painter Who Came in From the Cold." *Newsday* (New York), Apr. 25, 1972.

Genauer, Emily. "Art and the Artist." *New York Post*, Apr. 29, 1972.

*"Realist Art Master Returns." *Times-News* (Erie, Pa.), May 29, 1972.

*Winship, Frederick M. "Critics hostile but Levine oils back in vogue." *Boston Globe*, May 31, 1972.

Chapin, Louis. "Humane American Satirist." *Christian Science Monitor*, July 13, 1972.

Werner, Alfred. "Jack Levine: A Social Realist." *Jewish News* (Newark, N.J.), Feb. 6, 1975.

Glueck, Grace. "Paintings by Levine Defy Abstract Trend." *The New York Times*, Nov. 11, 1975.

Spencer, Charles. "Artists with a Social Conscience. Jack Levine: Painter of American Life." *Jewish Chronicle Literary Supplement* (New York), Dec. 5, 1975.

*Mosher, Charlotte. "Jewish Art Exhibition Offers Memorable Work." *Houston Chronicle*, Mar. 5, 1976.

*"Jack Levine: Retrospective Exhibit." *Jewish Advocate* (New York) Nov. 2, 1978.

*Russell, John S. "A Retrospective Show of Radical Art of Jack Levine." *The New York Times*, Nov. 11, 1978.

*Shenker, Israel. "Jack Levine Paintings at the Jewish Museum." *The New York Times*, Nov. 18, 1978.

*Tallmer, Jerry. "Graphics brood into the savage." *New York Post* Nov. 25, 1978.

*Werner, Alfred. "Levine Retrospective Praised as MOMA Features Matisse." *The Jewish News* (Newark, N.J.), Dec. 7, 1978.

*Szonyi, David. "I Swing a Heavy Brush." *Baltimore Jewish Times*, Jan. 5, 1979.

*Taylor, Robert. "Boston Expressionists: They marched to the beat of a different drummer." *Boston Sunday Globe*, Jan. 14, 1979.

*Holmes, Ann. "Levine loves being 'singular in my time.'" *Houston Chronicle*, Sept. 17, 1979.

Steiner, Raymond J. "Profile on Jack Levine." *Art Times* (Mount Marion, N.Y.), November 1985, pp. 8–9.

Jones, Marvin. "Jack Levine: Social Commentator." *The New Common Good* (New York, N.Y.), September 1986, pp. 1–9, and October 1986, pp. 1–9.

Giuliano, Charles. "A Conversation with Jack Levine." *Art New England* (Newtonville, Mass.), October 1986, pp. 6–8.

"Renowned Artist Has Exhibit at Hebrew College." *Jewish Advocate* (Boston), Oct. 29, 1987, p. 20.

FILMS (arranged chronologically)

Jack Levine, by Zina Voynow, Peter Robinson, and Herman J. Engel, 1963, produced by Zina Voynow.

Jack Levine: Feast of Pure Reason, produced and directed by David Sutherland, 1985.

Index

abstract art, 8, 10
Abstract Expressionism, 8, 11, 12, 50, 54, 127
Alan, Charles, 71, 97; The Alan Gallery, 71, 97
Alberti (istoria), 8, 19
Amsterdam, 114
Ashcan school, 10
avant-garde art, 10, 111
Beckmann, Max, 14, 20
The Beggar's Opera (John Gay), 13
Bellini, Giovanni, 108
Bernstein, Leonard, 93
Blitzstein, Marc, 14, 93
Bloom, Hyman, 19, 20, 23, 127
Botticelli, Sandro, 32
Braque, Georges, 20, 50
Capote, Truman, 106
Cézanne, Paul, 8, 20, 34
Chagall, Marc, 20
Communism, 11, 13, 41, 64
Cranach, Lucas, 54
Cubism, 8, 11, 20, 51, 53, 54, 108
da Settignano, Desiderio, 93
Daumier, Honoré, 13, 91
da Vinci, Leonardo, 8, 25, 108
Davis, Stuart, 34
Degas, Edgar, 25, 89, 97, 126
Depression, 9–11, 14, 50, 93, 126
distortion, 26, 30–33, 128
Donatello, 93
Downtown Gallery, 21, 34
Dreigroschenoper. See *The Threepenny Opera*
Dürer, Albrecht, 136
Dutch painting, 50, 54
Eastern Europe, 36, 45, 125, 137; Prague, 45, 125
Eisenstein, Sergei, 8
El Greco, 12, 32, 44, 92, 95, 108
Evergood, Philip, 11, 41
Expressionism, 8, 14, 20, 25, 31, 32, 44, 52, 103
Fascism, 11, 13, 87; Franco's Spain, 87, 101; Hitler's Germany, 87, 112
Flemish painting, 37–38, 50, 54, 55
Fogg Art Museum, Harvard, 19, 25
Francesca, Piero della, 133
Fredenthal, David, 34
Gainsborough, Thomas, 94
Germany, 13, 20, 87, 100, 112
Gikow, Ruth. See Levine: wife
Gombrich, Ernest, 97
Goya, Francisco, 11, 13, 87, 108
Grosz, George, 13, 20, 87
Guttuso, Renato, 127
Hogarth, William, 13
Holbein, Hans, 25, 94, 100
Hollywood movies, 13, 95, 103, 115; gangster films, 13, 32, 35, 50, 59
Impressionism, 19, 83
Ingres, Jean August Dominique, 25
Israel, 7, 110; Jerusalem, 119, 120, 127. See also Levine: travels to Israel
Italy, 50; Naples, 8; Rome, 50–53, 92; Venice, 117
Judaica, 37, 38, 50, 54, 136. See also Levine: Judaism
Kokoschka, Oskar, 14, 20, 23, 108
Kuniyoshi, Yasno, 34
Last Supper (da Vinci), 8, 67
Lenya, Lotte, 82, 83, 97
Levine, Jack: the army, 8, 34, 36, 41, 42, 44, 97; the art world, 50, 110, 117, 127, 137, 138; Boston, 14, 15, 18, 23, 29, 35, 36, 40, 43, 46, 47, 59, 70, 94, 126; classical influence, 20, 34, 43, 44, 114; daughter (Susanna), 78, 79; father (Samuel), 22, 34, 37, 45; Guggenheim Fellowship, 34; Hebrew language, 18, 34, 36, 38, 50, 55, 120, 125, 127, 136; Judaism, 14, 34, 36, 38, 54, 93, 110, 125, 127, 134; mother, 18, 34, 37; New York, 34, 40, 50, 63, 79, 115, 138; painting techniques, 13, 32, 42, 44, 47; travels to Europe, 41, 44, 50–52, 92, 117; travels to Israel, 55, 93, 119, 125, 127, 134; wife (Ruth Gikow), 34, 44, 45, 78, 79, 92, 97, 106, 112, 119, 126, 127, 128
Levine, Jack, works by:
Drawings and studies:
    The Banquet, **40**
    Courtroom Study, **63**
    David and Saul, (study), **134**
    Discussion, **23**
    Election Night (study), **66**
    The Feast of Pure Reason (study), **29**
    First Draft for *Gangster Funeral*, **62**

Gangster Funeral (study), **58**
Gangster Funeral (study), **62**
Horse, **39**
Jewish Cantors in the Synagogue, **22**
Judgment of Paris (study), **103**
Mars Confounded (study), **43**
Medicine Man, **71**
Medicine Show, **71**
Medicine Show (study), **71**
Medicine Show III (study), **70**
The Mourner, **58**
The Mourner (study for *Gangster Funeral*), **59**
Neighborhood Physician (study), **31**
Opening Night—Man in a Top Hat (study for *For the Sake of Art*), **110**, 111
The Organ Grinder, **18**
Portrait of Kanji Nakamura, **20**
The Quartet, **24**
Reception in Miami (study), **48**
St. Jerome, **7**
Seated Nude Youth, **19**
Shammai (final draft study), **124**
Soviet Visitation in Jerusalem No. 7 (study), **119**
Soviet Visitation in Jerusalem No. 7 (study), **119**
Standing Woman (study for *Medicine Show*), **70**
Study of Harold Zimmerman, **19**
Paintings:
    The Abundant Life, **50**
    Adam and Eve (1951), **54**
    Adam and Eve (1959), **92**
    Adam and Eve (*Eve Offers the Apple to Adam*), **128**
    Adam and Eve (*Expulsion*), **128**
    Aid to Digestion, **40**
    Apteka, **46**
    Armorers, **133**
    The Arms Brokers, **132**, 133
    The Art Lover, **100**
    At the Precinct, **126**
    Auction, **137**, 138
    Bandwagon (Four More Years), **115**
    The Banquet (1941), **35**
    The Banquet (1954), **66**
    Beatnik Girl, **96**
    Bedroom Scene, **97**
    Birmingham '63, **98**, 100
    The Black Freighter, **83**
    Blue Angel, **97**
    The Boy David Playing the Harp, **93**
    Brain Trust (Conference), **23**
    Cafè, **96**
    Café Figaro, **96**
    Cain and Abel, 8, 128, **129**
    Card Game, **21**
    The Card Players, **34**
    The Card Players, **35**
    Carnival at Sunset, 83, **130**, 131
    Cigarette Girl, 66, **80**
    City Lights No. 1, **30**
    City Lights No. 2, **30**
    Daley's Gesture, **109**
    Danse Champêtre, **114**
    David and Saul, 134, **135**
    Dealer, **138**
    Dramatis Personae, **35**
    Election Night, **68**, 88
    Election Night II, **67**,
    Ethnikon, **118**
    Every Inch a Ruler (The End of the Line), **48**
    The Eye of the Beholder, **137**
    The Feast of Pure Reason, **9**, 12, 21, **28**, 29, 32, 52
    Fêtes Galantes, **114**
    For the Sake of Art—Avant Garde, **111**
    Gangster Funeral, 13, 50, 52, 59, **60**, 62–64, 126
    Gangster Funeral (detail), **61**
    Gangster Wedding, **62**
    Gentleman from the South, **40**
    Girl in Orange, **89**
    The Girls from Fleugel Street, 80, **81**
    The Golden Anatomy Lesson, 52, **53**
    The Great Society, **106**
    The Green Cloche, **97**
    Hillel, 54, **74**
    Homage to Boston 43, **47**
    Hong Kong Tailor, **112**
    Horse and Wagon, **39**
    The Humanist, **54**
    Inauguration, 50, **84**, 85
    Inauguration II, **85**
    L'Indifférent, **113**, 117
    In the Valley of Kidron, **134**
    Jacob Wrestling with the Angel, **125**
    Jocasta (The Infancy of an Art Critic), **116**, 117
    Judah, **75**
    The Judge, **64**, 85

The Judgment of Paris (Paris as a Greenwich Village Dreamer), **102**
The Judgment of Paris I, **103**
The Judgment of Paris II, **103**
The Judgment of Paris III (Paris as a Movie Director), 103, **104**
The Judgment of Paris IV (Paris Wearing a Phrygian Cap), 103, **104**
The Judgment of Paris V (The Artist as Himself as Paris), 103, **105**
The Judgment of Paris VI (Paris as a Fashion Photographer), 103, **105**
The King, **37**
King Asa, 55, **56**
King David, **55**
King David Playing the Harp, **37**
King Josiah, **37**
King Saul, 55, **56**
Kronos, **137**
Lady with Opera Glasses, **89**
The Last Waltz, **95**
Love, Oh Careless Love, **82**
Magic for the Millions, 44, **45**
Maimonides, 54, **55**
Man with Cigar, **106**
The Man with the Stained Glass Eye, **59**
Mars Confounded, **43**
Matron of the Arts, **116**
Matroneia, **117**
Medicine Show, **69**, 70–71, 131
Medicine Show I, **72**
Medicine Show IV, **73**
Mosca and Volpone, **116**, 117
Moses on Sinai, **127**
Nehemiah, **77**
Neighborhood Physician, **31**
Nighttown Scene, **21**
1932 (In Memory of George Grosz), **11**, 87
Noah Releasing Dove, **134**
Nude (Burlesque Dancer), **32**
Oak Street, **10**, **90**, 91
The Offering, **58**
Oh Moon of Alabama, **113**
Old Mortality, **126**
On the Block, 89, 138, **139**
Opening Night—Woman with a Fan, 110, **111**
Orpheus in Vegas, **131**, 137
Our Presence in the Far East, **113**
Panethnikon, 118, **122–123**
The Passing Scene, 22, **36**, 38
The Patriarch of Moscow on a Trip to Jerusalem, 8, 119, **121**
The Pawnshop, 50, **51**, 52, 54
The Pensionnaire, **38**
The Pink Hat, **89**
Planning King Solomon's Temple, **38**
Portrait of Ruth, **79**
Portrait of Susanna, **79**
The Princess, **94**
Rabbi from Prague, **124**, 125
Rabbi in White, **136**, 137
Reception in Miami, 8, 48, **49**
Reclining Nude, **82**
Reconstruction, **100**
The Reluctant Ploughshare, **42**
Rich Man, Poor Man, **33**
The Roaring Tropics, 106, **107**
Roaring Twenties, **115**
Sacrifice of Isaac, **124**, 125
Samson and the Lion, **136**
The Scribe, **76**
Self-Portrait at Westchester Party, **110**
The Senator, **85**
Shammai, **124**, 125
Shelomo, **22**, 55
Six Masters: A Devotion, **108**
The Spanish Prison, **11**, **101**
Stalingrad (The Age of Steel), **112**
The Street, 21, 26, **27**
Street Scene No. 1, **26**
Street Scene No. 2, **26**
String Quartet, **12**, **25**, 34
String Quartet No. 2, **24**
Susanna, **78**
Susanna as a Charro, **78**
The Syndicate, 14, **32**, 33
Texas Delegate, **109**
Thirty-five Minutes from Times Square, **80**
Three Graces, **91**
Titian Misremembered, **108**
Tombstone Cutter, **45**
The Trial, 8, 63, 64, **65**
The Turnkey, 82, **86**, 87
Under the El, **52**

Vineyards of Timnah, **136**
Visit from the Second World, 119, **120**
Volpone at San Marco, **116**, 117
Warrior's Return (Battle's End), 43, **44**
Welcome Home, 8, **41**, 42, 43
The White Horse, 38, **39**
Witches' Sabbath 8, **99**, 100
Woman of Sint Olafstraat, **114**
Woodstock Pastorale, **47**
Series:
    "The Judgment of Paris" series, 103
    kings and sages of Israel series, 22, 37, 47, 54, 55, 74–77
    "The Medicine Show" series, 68–73, 131
McCarthyism, 8, 11, 50, 64
"Magic Realism," 12
Maroger, Jacques, 47
Matisse, Henri, 34
Metropolitan Museum of Art, 12, 34, 50
Mexican frescoes, 8, 20
Michelangelo, 8, 32, 114; Sistine Chapel, 8, 92
Modernism, 10, 95
Mostel, Zero, 40
Mughal painting, 18, 37–38
Museum of Modern Art, 12, 21, 22, 50, 59
Mussorgsky, Modest, 20, 33; *Boris Godunov*, 20, 33; *Pictures at an Exhibition*, 33
Nast, Thomas, 13
Nazism, 112
New York, 14, 15, 45, 50, 83, 111, 138. See also Levine; New York
Old Masters, 7, 25, 47, 50, 55, 108, 114
Old Testament, 37, 54, 55, 92, 93, 110, 128, 134, 136
Oriental art, 8, 18, 19, 55, 87
Panofsky, Erwin, 38
Persian influence, 37, 38, 50, 54
Phillips Gallery, 21, 48
Picasso, Pablo, 20, 30, 51, 108, 127
Pollaiuolo, Antonio, 136
Portrait painting, 8, 78–79, 94, 97, 108, 110, 114, 137
Poussin, Nicolas, 34
Raeburn, Sir Henry, 29
Realism, 10, 11, 12, 13
Regionalism, 8, 10–12
Rembrandt van Rijn, 8, 12, 34, 44, 52, 91, 108, 114; *The Return of the Prodigal Son*, 8
Renaissance, 8, 19, 38, 50, 106, 120, 125, 134
Rockwell, Norman, 14, 50
Rosenberg, Julius and Ethel, 8, 64
Ross, Denman W., 18, 19
Rouault, Georges, 20, 23
royalty, 48, 94, 95, 100
Rubens, Peter Paul, 12, 13, 34, 47, 91, 92, 108, 131, 136
Saatchi, Charles and Doris, 127
School of Paris, 14, 19, 20, 54, 127
Shahn, Ben, 11, 34, 41, 109
Sheeler, Charles, 34
Siporin, Mitchell, 11, 34
Skowhegan School of Painting and Sculpture (Maine), 63
Social art, 9, 10
Social Realism, 8–13, 127
the South, 40, 100
Soutine, Chaim, 14, 20, 23, 33, 95
Soviet Union, 11, 110, 112; Russians, 41, 119, 120
Soyer Brothers (Moses, Raphael, Isaac), 10, 34; Raphael Soyer, 50, 85
Surrealism, 8, 11, 12
Sutherland, Graham, 108
The Threepenny Opera (Brecht & Weill), 13, 20, 50, 80, 83, 91, 97, 115
Time Magazine, 46, 109
Tintoretto, Jacopo, 8, 25, 32, 44
Titian, 12, 34, 92, 108, 109; *Rape of Europa*, 108
Uccello, Paolo, 134
Ulysses (Joyce), 29
van der Goes, Hugo, 54
Van der Weyden, Roger, 38
Van Dyke, Anthony, 94
Van Eyck, Jan, 38, 55
Van Gogh, Vincent, 97
Vatican, 8, 128, 134
Velázquez, Diego, 12, 13, 94, 108
Venetian style, 8, 13, 25
Vietnam, 113
Watteau, Antoine (*L'Indifférent*), 113
Whitney Museum, 127
Works Project Administration (WPA), 9, 11, 20–23, 25
World War II, 11, 34, 36, 100, 112, 127
Zimmerman, Harold, 18, 19